SURVIVORS

*Breaking the Silence on
Child Sexual Abuse*

Eirliani Abdul Rahman | Daniel Fung

Marshall Cavendish
Editions

Published by Marshall Cavendish Editions
An imprint of Marshall Cavendish International

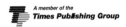
A member of the
Times Publishing Group

Other Marshall Cavendish Offices:
Marshall Cavendish Corporation. 99 White Plains Road, Tarrytown NY 10591-9001, USA • Marshall Cavendish International (Thailand) Co Ltd. 253 Asoke, 12th Flr, Sukhumvit 21 Road, Klongtoey Nua, Wattana, Bangkok 10110, Thailand • Marshall Cavendish (Malaysia) Sdn Bhd, Times Subang, Lot 46, Subang Hi-Tech Industrial Park, Batu Tiga, 40000 Shah Alam, Selangor Darul Ehsan, Malaysia

Marshall Cavendish is a registered trademark of Times Publishing Limited

National Library Board, Singapore Cataloguing-in-Publication Data

Name(s): Eirliani Abdul Rahman. I Fung, Daniel, author.
Title: Survivors : breaking the silence on child sexual abuse / Eirliani Abdul Rahman, Daniel Fung.
Description: Singapore : Marshall Cavendish Editions, [2018]
Identifier(s): OCN 1006822994 I ISBN 978-981-47-9401-5 (paperback)
Subject(s): LCSH: Child sexual abuse. I Sexual abuse victims.
Classification: DDC 362.76--dc23

Printed in Singapore by Markono Print Media Pte Ltd

Image Credits:
All images courtesy of the respective contributors except page 99 (Eirliani Abdul Rahman).

Survivors of child sexual abuse suffer in silence. They often keep the abuse a secret for many years and may have been living with those memories for a long time. They may have tried to tell others and met with resistance or felt there was no one they could trust. For these reasons, they struggle with poor self-esteem and feelings of guilt, shame and blame. However, they must know that the abuse was not their fault and they are not alone. It is never too late to disclose their experience and start the healing process from the trauma.

Professor Ho Lai Yun
Director, Child Development Programme,
Ministry of Health, Singapore

This engaging and touching book definitely addresses a very real and significant issue of child sexual abuse. I applaud the efforts of the authors and the survivors who shared their stories. A very worthwhile read.

Dr. Lee Cheng
President,
Singapore Psychiatric Association

Having worked for close to three decades with both child victims and adult survivors of childhood sexual abuse, I am pained at the horrors that these writers of varying ages and from different countries have had to endure during their tender years. Yet, I am in deep awe at their resilience in having survived such profound trauma, and their courage in sharing their stories so that others who are abused will have hope in knowing they are not alone. We know that such devastating betrayal in reaching effects on adult relationships, self-identity and mental wellness, and I send them my prayers and wish them only the best in their individual healing journeys. May they continue to find safe, stable, and trustworthy folk who will walk alongside them on the road to wholeness and recovery.

Vivienne Ng
Chief Psychologist,
Ministry of Social and Family Development, Singapore

This book contains personal accounts of the experiences
of survivors of child sexual abuse.
Some readers may find the content disturbing.

CONTENTS

FOREWORD
Bernard Gerbaka

President, International Society for Prevention
of Child Abuse and Neglect (ISPCAN)

"I… always wanted people to… read my mind so that I wouldn't be misjudged. I think that happens way too often. I feel like there's a reason for why people do the things they do; the reasons may not be legitimate or excusable, but it's still an explanation. People always look at what lies on the surface, at the obvious. They rarely try to see deeper, the cause of it all, how it all happened. You can always trace things back to the beginning and find the unseen pieces that affected people's actions. I wish my parents took more time to analyse me as a child, so they could question themselves as to why all of a sudden, I had difficulties…"

Lucie (Chapter 10)

In this book, there are many testimonies, painful stories, typical scenarios and underestimated situations. Each child has a different experience of sexual abuse, either with a stranger or with a close relative; the consequences are often dramatic and overwhelming. They are rarely about physical scars; they are always about the image of oneself, the value it is given and the support it provides.

Most importantly, those stories bring to our conscience what our competences, potentials and duties are, as a coalition of diverse and experienced professionals working with children: to prevent child abuse and protect our children!

This is the core mission of the International Society for Prevention of Child Abuse and Neglect (ISPCAN).

Connecting more than 1,200 professionals in about 120 countries for the past 40 years, ISPCAN is a board member in the Global Partnership to End Violence Against Children, aiming at working for a better world for children. ISPCAN offers training materials to professionals globally and is enriched by membership cross-culturally, to better learn about the problem and its prevention, about professional intervention, about child and family empowerment: parenting is now a critical component of our INSPIRE WHO strategies. In current difficult times for displaced children, ISPCAN sustains and strengthens the global movement for child protection and shares material for expertise and tools for leadership and advocacy, globally, in a culturally sensitive manner.

Children matter most! Within supportive families, at the centre of a child-friendly system, they define our present as we carve their future. We owe them that much.

PREFACE

When I set out to chronicle the stories of these 12 brave men and women, survivors of child sexual abuse (CSA), I had no inkling of the road ahead. I did not expect these individuals to be so gifted in storytelling: they were lyrical, they were poignant, they were happy, they were sad. I was moved, not just by their bravery in sharing such a dark period in their lives, something which has left an indelible stamp on their beings. I was moved also by their desire to reach out to other survivors, to tell them that one day they will heal, even if today seems like being submerged in the darkest of pits. I admire their courage, more so because two in particular have chosen to use their real names, Imran and Sasha. And that four of them, Imran and Sasha included, have agreed to read excerpts of their respective chapters at book readings.

When I put out a call to friends in December 2014, asking to spread the word that I was looking to interview survivors of CSA, the recommendations came in fast and furious. Every survivor in the book was either a friend, or became one via word of mouth. I feel honoured and blessed that they had chosen to tell their story now, putting aside their fears and concerns that this may trigger emotional pain. They chose instead to look to the future, to show others that their journeys illuminate the light at the end of the proverbial tunnel. In the face of such fierce determination, I felt it my duty to reflect their voices in as true a light as possible, to show the multi-faceted side of each storyteller. So these stories are not all doom and gloom. There is plenty of wit, self-effacing irony, even laughter. There is peace too where there is closure. And, always, the hope that their stories will help others.

Child sexual abuse is not confined to any particular demographic segment of society: it can affect anyone, regardless of class or social status. More often, it is opportunistic, taking place because of the abuser's close proximity to the child, and it is also sometimes about the display of power and the asymmetry of power within a household. In this book, you will meet two young millennials, best friends in their early twenties, residing in Berlin: one was abused by a house help growing up, the other by a boyfriend. You will find a young lady from Singapore, born physically challenged and taken advantage of by her own father, and a woman who had been abused by her teacher and whose sister committed suicide many years later after having endured abuse at the hands of the same teacher as a child. You will encounter a woman in her early thirties from Myanmar, who was preyed on by a much older male cousin as a child, and another, now in her fifties from Britain, who fell into a child prostitution ring in her late teens after having been abused by her father. It is not the case that the perpetrators are all men. You will hear the stories of five men, two of whom were abused by their grandmothers and another by his mother. The 12 survivors hail from Germany, India, Indonesia, Myanmar, Singapore, South Africa, the UK and the US, of diverse backgrounds. Some of the abusers died before the survivors could come to terms with what had happened. Each chose their own path towards healing.

Each story is the voice of one survivor. Every teleconversation or meeting was about three hours long so that I could record verbatim what they said; any longer and it could be too draining. Here, I have put down only their side of the conversation, as if they are speaking directly to you, the reader, although in some places they addressed me using my nickname "Lin".

I marvel at their courage to describe all the horrifying details to make the picture as complete as possible. More than once, I felt sickened by the horrific abuse that these survivors had been through. On one occasion, I found it hard to transcribe my notes as the multiple abuses that this survivor had gone through really wrenched at my core. How can it be possible that human beings can be such beasts? But the light of hope from these survivors – that their valiant telling of their stories will help ease the pain of other survivors and their loved ones, and help point the way towards healing – renews me every time I read what they have sent me, be it lyrics, poetry or verse. I honour their commitment to this book.

To paraphrase Ralph Waldo Emerson: to know that one life has breathed easier, this is to have lived.

Eirliani Abdul Rahman
September 2017
Colorado, US

PART I: STORIES

1

SASHA

Sasha Joseph Neulinger, now 28, was sexually abused by two uncles and a cousin as a child. The abuse began when he was four years old and ended after he told his mother when he was eight. The next nine years were spent in court testifying against his abusers, the toll of which led him to become suicidal. One uncle and the cousin were put behind bars, while the other pleaded guilty and was sentenced to 12 years of probation.

In April 2014, Sasha launched a Kickstarter Campaign for "Rewind To Fast-Forward", an autobiographical documentary surviving multigenerational child sexual abuse. Raising over US$176,000 from over 4,395 backers, "Rewind To Fast-Forward" became the 6th most backed documentary in Kickstarter history. After digitising over 200 hours of home video, Sasha directed an Emmy Award-winning crew in his hometown, interviewing his mother, father, sister, detective, prosecutor, and psychiatrist for a three-week film shoot. Sasha also travels the United States as a motivational speaker for reforms in child advocacy and child protection. His TEDxBozeman talk entitled "Trauma is irreversible. How it shapes us is our choice" (www.youtube.com/watch?v=K_WL5iqvPlY) has been viewed more than 150,000 times. In 2016, Sasha founded his own public speaking company, Voice For The Kids, LLC.

a teleconversation, Bozeman, Montana
6th March 2016

RAPED

I grew up in Rosemont, Pennsylvania, just outside Philadelphia. It was a nice middle-class suburban area. Beautiful Victorian houses, safe streets, and beautiful mature trees and foliage. Our house was big, with a wonderful wraparound deck and a spacious front and backyard. I'm sure everything appeared normal from the outside, and certainly no outsider would have assumed that it wouldn't be a safe place for children.

When people think about child sexual abuse, I think it is easier for them to imagine a creepy man in a white van, or a dirty stranger kidnapping a child from a schoolyard or abusing them remotely. It's easier for people to jump to the conclusion that child abusers are people who we don't know.

My uncle Howard was a well-trusted and well-respected Jewish cantor who was the first cantor to sing for the Pope at the Vatican in 1992, and who sang for the highly well-respected and largest synagogue in Manhattan, New York, Temple Emanu-El. My uncle Larry was always the life of the party and was great at making people laugh, and my cousin Stewart was a military veteran who had served his country in the United States Air Force. All three men raped me multiple times. At least in the United States, in 80 percent or more of child sexual abuse cases, the child is abused by someone he or she knows and trusts.

UNCLE HOWARD

When I was four years old, I was raped for the first time, by my Uncle Howard, although this was not the first time that he had abused me. The pain was excruciating and I couldn't understand why it was happening. It felt like with every second, a part of me was being murdered, like a part of my consciousness was dying. I was turning off inside, surrendering vital pieces of my soul in exchange for each breath.

I had never been so confused. The confusion was a murky cloud that engulfed me along with the pain, which made it hard to breathe. I wanted to cry, I wanted to scream, and I wanted my life to be over if the pain wouldn't stop. I couldn't cry; I couldn't talk.

I was paralysed.

I remember that as this was happening, I started to find a numbness. I came to the point where all I could feel was my body moving back and forth, yet I couldn't feel it anymore.

I remember focusing on the blue fibres of the carpet in my room. I could feel my face rubbing against the carpet. I could feel my heart beating and my mind becoming very quiet.

When it was over, I wasn't able to exit this emotional numbness. I was in a quiet space, but filled with fear. It was like when he raped me, he took a part of who I was.

I didn't expect this kind of pain with my Uncle Howard. I didn't understand why somebody who I loved and trusted would inflict that kind pain on me. If my uncle could do this to me, I must have done something wrong and I deserved it. I was dirty, disgusting, and unlovable. That is what I believed as a four-year-old boy who had been raped, and I have worked my whole life to change that belief about myself.

The most notable and terrifying moment of all of the abuse I endured came from my Uncle Howard during Thanksgiving at my home in Rosemont, Pennsylvania.

The whole family was there, and my mom, who is an incredible chef, cooked and baked so much food that to my four-year-old eyes, it looked as though there was enough food for 50 people. I remember the turkey was being carved, and the turkey leg was a coveted piece of the turkey in our family, so I let the whole table know that I wanted a turkey leg. One was already assigned to somebody in the family – I don't remember who – so there was only one left. Howard wanted it.

We were in the dining room. On one end, there was a swinging door to the pantry, and on the other, there was an open archway to the living room. Shortly after I had informed the table that I wanted a turkey leg, I left my seat to play with my toys in the pantry. My Uncle Howard followed me.

Today, I believe that what happened in that room was a power play. A show of dominance. Despite the family being on the other side of the door, he had no fear of being caught.

He grabbed the head of my penis between the flesh of his thumb and his finger. He pinched my penis, clenched his teeth and told me that he wanted the last turkey leg and that it was his. Then he threatened me. "If you tell anyone," he said, his teeth still clenched, "I'll kill you."

The scar from that pinch is still visible today.

I was terrified that night. His deep baritone voice while his fingers pinched me was so traumatising that it took over a decade of therapy to heal from that moment. He got that turkey leg. I was so scared of my Uncle Howard, and I would do whatever he said.

"Let's go play in your room," he'd say. I would say, "OK." If I didn't agree, he'd kill me: that was what I believed as a child victim of sexual abuse.

UNCLE LARRY

My Uncle Larry was always someone who made me laugh. I was fond of him, and in many ways he reminded me of my dad because he was funny and charismatic. We would be goofing around together and before the abuse started, we had a lot of fun together. I wasn't scared of him, and never had a reason to believe that I should be.

One day, my Uncle Larry and I were playing in my room – this was after Howard had already started abusing me – and he invited me to play a game that he called the "Lollipop" game. And then he licked my penis, sodomised me fully and put his finger in my butt. It was so confusing because it was not as painful as what Howard had been doing to me, but it was still extremely uncomfortable. When he was doing this, he smiled at me with a sad look in his eyes, almost as if he was worried that he might be hurting me.

Imagine the confusion when I walked down the stairs after moments of abuse, only to watch my abusers hug my parents and grab a piece of pie, or a beer, and go about the day as if nothing out of the ordinary had happened. I started to wonder if my parents knew what my abusers were doing to me and were okay with their actions. My Uncle Larry would hug my mom and grab a piece of the pie that she had made. I'd come down from being abused and there would be smiles from my dad and mom at my abuser. It only added to my isolation and self deprecating beliefs about myself.

DIRTY, DISGUSTING AND UNLOVABLE

I thought I was being abused because I was dirty, disgusting and unlovable. By the time I was seven, I was being abused by Larry, Howard and Stewart on separate and multiple occasions. There was no fight at all because I thought they were supposed to do that to me. I thought this was supposed to happen because I deserved it.

Larry's son, my cousin Stewart, moved in with us after being honourably discharged from the United States Air Force. From what I understood, he was having trouble with drugs, but, just like with Howard and Larry, my parents never suspected that he would abuse me. His own parents wouldn't take him in, and so out of "love" for their struggling nephew, my parents opened our home to him.

I thought he was someone I could trust, although "trust" was a relative term for me at that point. He'd play football with me in front of our house, pick me up and hold me upside-down, make funny faces at me. He was very strong because he was in the military. He'd pick me up and spin me around and I can remember how much I would laugh when he did that.

When Howard abused me, I was surprised. When Larry abused me, I was surprised. When Stewart started abusing me, it was even more surprising because he was even nicer to me than my Uncle Larry. My trust in adults was so fragile; my self-esteem was… My world felt like a dark and evil place because I believed I was dirty, disgusting and unlovable.

DISCLOSURE

I was prepared to accept my life for the awful, painful, anxiety-provoking experience that it was.

One day, Stewart called me up to his room in the attic for another session. As I walked up the stairs towards him, I saw my little sister exit his room. I slowed my pace, and as I continued to walk up the stairs towards her, she began to walk down the stairs towards me. As I got closer I could hear the repressed squeakiness of her sobs. I could see the flushed redness in her cheeks. As we locked eyes, I could see her tears. We stared at each other in the middle of the stairwell.

Up until that very moment I had believed that my abusers were hurting me, and ONLY me because I was dirty, disgusting, and unlovable. But my sister? My sweet, beautiful baby sister was the most beautiful person in my life, and I couldn't understand how or why anyone would hurt her.

It was in that moment that I finally realised that what my abusers were doing was wrong. My sister didn't deserve to be hurt, and maybe, just maybe, I didn't deserve to be hurt either.

I knew that my sister wouldn't say anything and I wanted my parents to know everything. I didn't know if it was just Stewart, or if Larry and Howard were also abusing my sister, but I wanted it to stop. My sister saved my life, because on that stairwell, she instantly shattered my belief that what was happening was only happening to me, because I was dirty, disgusting and unlovable.

That night, I told my mom that Stewart had a secret club in his room where he and my sister did "Bad Things". My mom tried to get more information from my sister, who was scared to open up. Could you blame her?

To be fair, my mom wasn't passive about this. For the period I was being abused, she became certain something was wrong. I was in the hospital a lot as I had rectal bleeding. She went to the school, spoke to the teachers, and made the school agree that no one faculty member was allowed to be alone with me. I always had to be accompanied by a minimum of two adults at school. She never expected her two brothers-in-law and her nephew to be the culprits.

Shortly after telling my mom about the "secret club", I had an anxiety-provoked breakdown. I believed that my abusers could see every step that I took, and that they could hear every thought in my mind, and that they were already plotting my death simply for hinting about what was happening to my sister.

I grabbed a piece of underwear from my room, along with a Sharpie. I wrote on the underwear: "I spoiled brat", "I'm a bitch", "I suck", "I am a loser". I cut out two holes for my eyes, put it on my head and wore it like a mask. I then went downstairs – naked – with this mask on.

My sister, my mom and Stewart were in the kitchen. I grabbed a kitchen knife, put it to my neck and I started screaming at the top of my lungs.

So you can imagine this: my mom had just found out from her son that there might be abuse, she's having a discussion with Stewart, and then I come downstairs with this underwear mask, naked, and now I have a knife – a big knife – against my neck.

Stewart comes over and said, "Stop! You don't want to do this." I looked at him and screamed and screamed at him.

He left the room, packed his bags and left the house. He never came back. He left without saying anything. He just left.

SILENCE WAS BROKEN

It was that moment with my sister on the stairwell that set my eventual disclosure in motion, and it was my love for her that gave me the strength to break the silence.

My mom called the therapist I had at the time. He was on the phone with me, trying to calm me down. When the situation had been defused and I had put down the knife, the therapist told my mom, "I think you will need to go to a better therapist or even a psychiatrist. I'm not qualified for this. This is serious."

My mom had a friend at the Children's Hospital in Philadelphia, and she called him for help. We went to the hospital and he met me and my mom in the parking lot. He looked at me and said something to the effect of, "If you promise not to kill yourself, I'll promise to find you a good doctor to talk to – he will help you feel better and you will be safe."

He found us Dr. Herbert Lustig, the child psychiatrist who aided me in my healing process for over a decade. Dr. Lustig is one of my biggest heroes and is a huge reason why I am where I am today.

I was suffering from insomnia, which only aggravated my paranoia and suicidal thoughts. Dr. Lustig started me on medication that helped me to sleep, and once I was able to rest and reclaim stability, he was able to gain my trust and help me believe that I was safe in his office. I began to open up. I started by drawing a picture.

TALKING

After drawing multiple pictures, I began to talk about the abuse as well. The first time, I talked about my Uncle Larry and the "Lollipop" game. That was the first disclosure because he was the least scary of all. Then I talked about Stewart as he was the second scariest abuser. Then I talked about Howard.

I thought that the nightmare was over after I told Dr. Lustig and my parents the truth. They told me that it wasn't my fault and that what my abusers had done was awful, so I thought it was all over. Little did I know that for the next nine years of my life, I would be in and out of courtrooms, testifying against all three of my abusers.

KILLING MYSELF

I was asked to testify in court against all three of my abusers. It was a decision that I made because I didn't want my sister to be hurt again, but also because with the new knowledge that what they did was wrong and awful, I was now angry and wanted justice.

Though I wanted to testify, it was extremely difficult for me, and sometimes the fear of my abusers' threats, particularly Howard's, was enough to push me towards suicide. I feared that death from my Uncle Howard would be a million times more painful than if I just jumped out of a moving car, which I did in an attempt to take my own life when I was just eight years old. Suffering from PTSD, extreme anxiety and depression, I would also cut myself and bang my head hard against the floor. I was really suffering. That is what people need to understand... the abuse and rape is painful, yes, but the psychological and emotional pain that follows is oftentimes worse than the abuse itself.

The prosecution process took nine years mostly because Howard had a four-lawyer defence team that was paid for by members of the congregation at Temple Emanu-El. They had the money to delay, delay and delay in the hopes of tiring me out before we could get to a trial. The trauma of those nine years was second only to that of being raped.

At the time, Montgomery County, Pennsylvania, where my case was being prosecuted, did not have a Child Advocacy Center (CAC) to help me through the process.

Child Advocacy Centers provide a safe, child friendly environment where the child's official disclosure is filmed for later use by the prosecutors. The child is interviewed by a specially trained forensic interviewer, and while the interview is being conducted, it is being transmitted live on a monitor in another room where law enforcement, social services and mental health professionals, as well as prosecutors are watching. If any one of these team members needed to ask a question of the child, they would do so through the forensic interviewer so that the child only has to tell their traumatic story of abuse to ONE adult, not four or five. Importantly, the child only has to tell their story ONCE because if anyone needed to hear it again, they could simply watch the video of that interview.

When I was a child, we did not have a CAC, so before I even reached the stand of my first trial, I had been asked by child protection services, physicians, detectives and prosecutors to retell and relive my story over and over again. It was incredibly traumatic to travel all over the county and tell my story to all these adults in all these strange buildings, to relive and retell the most horrific moments of my life.

When I look back, when I speak now on child advocacy and the work of the CAC, I realise the amount of trauma I suffered by not having a CAC. I became exhausted from telling my story again and again. Also, it limited the effectiveness of my therapy with Dr. Lustig, because we spent too much time working on keeping me stable while the prosecution process was underway. It was hard to really dig deep into some of the core issues because I was working so hard just to remain upright from the exhaustion of prosecution. The trial process slowed the healing process, without a doubt.

THE FIRST DOMINO TO FALL

My Uncle Larry was the first domino to fall. After he went to the police station and failed his polygraph test, he confessed to what he had done, and also talked about his childhood and that he had been raped as a child by his older brother, my Uncle Howard. Larry's lawyer tried to get him to take back his confession but he ended up with 11 years in prison.

Stewart saw what happened to his dad and asked for a plea bargain shortly thereafter.

In my 2014 interview with Detective Ohrin, I learnt that Stewart talked about how he was abused by his father Larry. So we are starting to see a pattern here: multigenerational child sexual abuse. It should also be noted that after I told Dr. Lustig what had happened to me, my dad finally felt safe enough to reveal what had happened during his childhood: Larry and Howard had abused him in the very same way they abused me. This was a multigenerational child sexual abuse case that led all the way back to Howard.

UNCLE HOWARD

After successful trials against my Uncle Larry and my cousin Stewart, it was time to go after Howard but as stated earlier, Howard had four lawyers and an endless stream of money.

His defence fund was put together by members of Temple Emanu-El. The Temple Emanu-El chose not to believe my testimony, but instead backed their cantor, despite both my father and my Uncle Larry saying that Howard had abused them as children. When we went after Howard, Larry and my dad were going to testify against Howard in court. Howard appealed every court all the way to the Pennsylvania Supreme Court, and it took a long time. They decided my dad and Larry couldn't testify.

This was because of the statute of limitations.[1] It's so fucked up, and something that I am working to change with the work that I am doing as a public speaker and with my film. There is no statute of limitations for murder and there should not be for rape!

My dad and my Uncle Larry's testimonies were nails in Howard's coffin, but once the Pennsylvania Supreme Court overturned the ruling that my dad and Uncle Larry could testify, those nails were gone. Still, I was ready to face Howard in court, and my testimony and the evidence was strong enough on their own.

Howard's defence team had one strong tactic: DELAY AT ALL COSTS. Early on, his lawyers asked to see my testimonials, all the various forensic interviews that I had been asked to give. If you ask an eight-year-old child after the most traumatic experience in his life – being raped – to tell his story again and again, and AGAIN, there will be slight discrepancies in each telling of the story, not only in the eight-year-old's testimony, but in the notes taken by the different men and women in the plethora of fields who needed my case details.

The lawyers said: "Sasha is an actor," or "Sasha had many concussions playing hockey," or "He's been in therapy for so long," so "Maybe Sasha isn't a credible witness because he's not right in the head," and they used these multiple interviews against me. The court saw through that tactic, but it ate at the clock and chiseled away at my childhood.

They had enough funds to appeal and delay until I was nearly 17 years old. This was how long it took from the time

---

1   This forbids prosecution for offences that were committed more than a specified number of years ago. After the statutory period for the offence has run out, the alleged criminal cannot face criminal charges.

I disclosed at age 8! Can you believe that? When they ran out of delay tactics, the Howard camp quickly asked for a plea bargain, as they did not want to go to trial.

Risa Ferman, the District Attorney who was prosecuting my case, said to me that she thought we could win, but she could not give me an exact date of when the trial would end, and with the knowledge of Howard's unlimited financial resources, it was made clear that it could take years for a conviction. Howard had the resources to appeal indefinitely.

I'll get to the point: we had been doing this for nine years. I wanted to move on with my life. The thought of having a trial with Howard, going through the same bullshit... This trial could have gone on into my twenties, and he had already taken so many years of my life.

My need for him to "pay" for what he did left me vulnerable because at the time I believed my happiness could only be achieved by a conviction. In my rage towards him, I wanted him to be in prison and to be raped in prison. I had so much anger. I could spend another four years and not get the verdict I wanted.

I decided that I wanted to move on with my life, without my happiness hinging on a court ruling that could not be guaranteed. Furthermore, I wanted to make sure that he did not get away with a clean record – I wanted the world to know he was a child sexual abuser. That he sexually abused me.

We reached a plea bargain. In exchange for dropping the two felony charges, Howard pleaded guilty to five counts of child abuse misdemenours including indecent assault, terroristic threats, simple assault, corruption of minors and endangering the welfare of children.

It should be noted that in many states, there is no such thing as a child sexual abuse misdemeanour. Pennsylvania was behind the times, and still is along with many other states in the US. For the record, indecent assault, one of Howard's crimes, means that an adult exposes a child (me) to bodily fluids.

To this day, as I travel the country speaking for reforms in child advocacy, including laws like the statute of limitations, I don't understand how indecent assault is simply a misdemenour. And it's Pennsylvania state law! If you even pat a child the wrong way in the state of Texas, for example, you'd get 25 years minimum. If it had happened in Texas, it would have been a felony.

In any event, I got my day in court and I got to read my victim impact statement, in which I called Howard a coward to his face. It was a huge stepping stone in my journey to overcome the chains of my childhood abuse.

MOVING FORWARD

Just over a year after my final court appearance, I moved across the country to Bozeman, Montana, where I would study film production over the next four years, while also trying desperately to move on with my life. From age 4 to age 17, abuse was the primary focus of my existence, and so it took time to come down from the chaos I had lived through for the majority of my life.

I got a ton of help from my family and from Dr. Lustig, and despite all that had happened, I was functional, given every chance to move forward with my life. In my first semester at Montana State University, I scored a GPA of 4.0, and I enjoyed the beauty of the Montana wilderness, fishing, hiking and camping whenever I could. What was difficult was making the transition from being a child victim to an adult [male] survivor.

SEXUAL INTIMACY

I'm a heterosexual male. Like any young adult, I was interested in exploring my sexuality, and while I was good at flirting, I was terrified of being intimate with a woman. As soon as a woman would express interest in me, as soon as there was an opportunity for intimacy, I'd start pushing them away.

When I was able to overcome that obstacle, I found that I was choosing toxic partners who were emotionally abusive. Those experiences with women and dating were painful, but an important part of my journey towards understanding what was still wounded inside of me – helping me to become aware of my pain, and work towards healing.

I've learnt that if something in my life is bothering me, whether it be a person or a situation, I have to look inward and ask: Why am I engaging with this person or this experience? Because if it's not serving me in a healthy and positive way, why should I engage? If you're in an abusive relationship, why are you choosing to be with that person?

Questions for oneself.

a teleconversation, Bozeman, Montana
10th March 2016

UNHEALED WOUNDS

Even though I spent nine years in the court rooms, testifying against all three of my abusers, I had so much support. My parents supported me. My grandparents supported me. I also had 10 years of intensive psychotherapy. Even with all the support and love that was showered on me, there would still be unhealed wounds within me.

Pieces that could only be discovered in adulthood.

As a child, I was able to get a decent amount of closure and healing through testifying against my abusers, and working on coming to peace with what had happened to me; but there's still a difference between the social experience and interpersonal dynamics that you experienced as a child, compared to what you experience as an adult. So trust issues, intimacy and boundary awareness – these types of experiences are different for a child, compared to an adult. That transition from being a child victim to an adult survivor led to some challenges that I've had to face.

I thought, as an adult when I went away to college, that I had faced my demons and it was time to move on with my life. However, I felt I had to completely disconnect from my past to do that. What that meant to me was – at all costs – to never let anyone know what had happened to me. I thought if anyone knew about my past, they'd see me as dirty or disgusting or unlovable.

IMPENETRABLE MANLINESS

That led to falsehood – a false persona and an ego. I lifted a lot of weights. I shaved my head with a razor. I had a goatee. I wore a leather jacket. I wanted to project an image of impenetrable manliness. I didn't want people to see or perceive any weakness. I wanted to present an image that deterred anyone from feeling comfortable enough to dig deeper into who I was.

What I didn't realise then but what I understand now, is that I was still living in fear. I was very self-conscious. I would project this image of a grizzly, tough, intimidating, muscular man. But inside, I was so deeply insecure and terrified of intimacy. I had a lot of work ahead of me to get over that.

Sex was challenging for me. Any time I engaged in sexual activity, I'd feel guilty because of my role as a male in the heterosexual dynamic. Because I was the one who "inserted", I felt dirty for "penetrating". It was my own mental noise that had followed me from my childhood, preventing me from enjoying sex because I felt like an abuser even though it was consensual! I had the feeling there must be something wrong with her if she wanted to have sex with me. She must not be in her right mind!

So that belief system led me to self-sabotage: I would reject any opportunity for a healthy relationship. If there was a nice, well-rounded girl, I immediately was turned off because I thought she was crazy. How could I believe that someone could love me when I couldn't even love myself? And on the other side of the spectrum, I was very attracted to women who were unstable and emotionally abusive. You know, I believe that somewhere deep down inside – it all goes back to the decision when I left for college – that I had to abolish the past and create a new identity. That didn't serve me well at all.

That decision alienated me from myself, prevented me from having any opportunity of truly loving myself. I resented the child inside of me who was still scared and in need of self-love and nurturing. During my childhood, I had other adults to give me that love and nurturing, but as an adult, I had to learn how to give that love and nurturing to myself.

TOUGH GUY

The last trial ended the day before my 17th birthday. About six months later, I lost my virginity.

She was my first girlfriend, and it was my first sexual experience with a girl. She too was a victim of abuse as a child. We were together for a year and before I left for college, she ended up cheating on me. It was so, so devastating even though I was a young person. What I've realised over time is that I had a tendency to be attracted to deeply wounded women, women who had been abused. I mean, they didn't tell me so at the beginning but I'd always find out eventually.

It was an unspoken attraction of two victims to each other. Two people who were walking with unhealed wounds.

I was cheated on in high school and then I went to college. I didn't allow myself to focus on sex. For six years, I was celibate, even though it completely contradicted my "tough guy" persona. There were a lot of women who were attracted to me, whom I'd flirt with. But as soon as they wanted to be fully intimate with me, I'd stop talking to them. I'd push them away. I was scared.

For six years, I didn't really date. I flirted. I put on this image of confidence but it was ego-based, fear-based. I grew tired of that – the energy that it took to be someone I wasn't. But at the same time, I didn't know who I was. I just knew that I wasn't who I was pretending to be.

And so by my senior year of college, I started to let go of that tough guy persona. I started to change and soften a little bit. I started to spend more time in the back country of the Montana wilderness. I started talking to more people. I made some meaningful friends as well.

All of a sudden, I started to experience healthier relationships. I was still choosing unhealthy people but it wasn't *all* unhealthy. I was having this mix in my life.

DOCUMENTARY FILM-MAKING

I still struggled at times to create healthy boundaries with people, but I was starting to move in a healthier direction, and I was certainly aware of the work I needed to do to heal that blockage within myself. In my senior year of college, I was fortunate enough to get a job in a non-profit organisation called Big Sky Youth Empowerment. My job was to do a documentary-style video about the programmes that help to provide open conversation and counselling for troubled youth while enjoying the great outdoors.

While interviewing these kids, I was inspired by their openness, their bravery and their willingness to look at the challenges of their past. I quickly realised that I wanted to become a documentary filmmaker. Big Sky Youth Empowerment had an influential and well-respected board of directors, one of whom was Thomas Winston, who is now the Executive Producer of my film. Another is Rich Hahn, who is the Marketing Manager for Simms Fishing Products, a big company in Bozeman.

Thomas Winston and Rich Hahn both saw the film that I did for Big Sky Youth Empowerment. Thomas then asked me to work as a production assistant on his National Geographic Show, *America The Wild*, and simultaneously, I was asked by Simms Fishing Products to start producing marketing videos for them. Very quickly, before I had even graduated from college, I had two firm jobs which were really steady and brought a ton of experience.

EPIPHANY

About six months into working for Thomas – his company is called Grizzly Creek Films – I had a moment when I was at the editing bay. I felt pressure behind my eyes like I was about to cry. I had this moment of clarity: I love my life. I love the work that I get to do every day. I love the friends that I have – like Robert Schneeweis and Jeff Dougherty (also my current business partner and Director of Photography for my film) – and I was starting to learn what it felt like to love myself. At that moment, I thought I was fully loving myself. When I look back, what I see is that I was *learning* to love myself. I realised how much love I had received and benefited from in my life, how fortunate I was to be in that editing bay, after everything that I've been through. Three abusers and nine years of court trials, but somehow, I have survived.

That's what I felt: if I didn't tell my story, then I would be wasting an incredible opportunity to give back to all those survivors and all of those human beings who had gone through or are going through, child sexual abuse.

I called my dad and asked him, "Do you still have all those home videos?"

He said, "Yeah, I do."

I asked him to send them to me and he did. During the day, I'd work on the National Geographic show, and in the evenings I would sit in the editing bay with Robert and Jeff. We'd watch those tapes – those 200 hours of my childhood.

I watched some of the most beautiful moments of my life, moments that I had completely forgotten about because they had been overshadowed by the painful moments. I also watched my abusers interacting with me as a kid.

This footage gave me a more well-rounded perspective of my childhood and jumpstarted my healing as I got to see myself as a beautiful child. For the first time I got to see the beauty that *did* exist in my childhood. I got to see a beautiful child who was so sweet and just struggling through an awful situation that clearly wasn't his fault. It gave me an opportunity to actively see myself as a child through the eyes of an adult. I was 23 years old at the time.

STEP 1 FILMS

After I started looking at the tapes, I left my job with Thomas, with Grizzly Creek Films; started my own film production company with Robert and Jeff, flew to Philadelphia with the little savings that I had, and started filming *Rewind To Fast-Forward*.

We put together a pitch video of what we wanted to do with this film. Thomas watched it and asked if we were interested in his help.

Leaving Grizzly Creek Films was the bravest moment of my young career and the bravest moment of my young adult life, as I had dropped everything to seek the deepest truth within myself by exploring my past with openness. I went back to working with Grizzly Creek Films within six months after I had left, but instead of working as a production assistant, I was working as the Director of my own film, collaborating with Tom, who became the Executive Director. Things started rolling from there.

More than a year later, we had a successful Kickstarter: our film became the sixth most backed documentary in Kickstarter's history. With that, we were able to go back to Philadelphia with an Emmy Award-winning crew and film for three weeks. I was able to interview my mom, my dad, my psychiatrist, the prosecutor, and I was able to visit Mission Kids, the Child Advocacy Centre created in my county because of my case.

VULNERABLE

Right after the Kickstarter campaign, I entered my first relationship since high school. I had sex for the first time in six years. I felt comfortable for the first time. With the Kickstarter success, I was sharing my story with the world. It was a 180-degree turn from the weightlifting man with the goatee that I was telling you about earlier.

I was in my first relationship in six years. I had a lot of catching up to do in the lessons of dating because I had spent so much time alienating myself from intimacy. I had to learn the hard way about boundaries, earned trust, and the difference between co-dependency and a heathy relationship.

I was definitely on the path to facing my fear and growing as a human being. There were growing pains as we started to make the film. I had gotten myself to a place where I could be intimate, but I was still choosing unhealthy partners. The first woman I dated after Kickstarter had a traumatic childhood as well, and also suffered from the challenges of dealing with bipolar disorder. When we met, she was so open and present with me; and then a month in, she had a shift, and was immediately disinterested in me, became emotionally abusive, and started spending a lot of time with her ex-boyfriend. It was very, very painful, especially given the circumstances of my journey.

She eventually cheated on me, and ultimately I had to step back and ask myself how I missed the red flags and why I chose her as my partners (this opened the door to tremendous growth later in my journey towards healing and fully loving myself).

The day after we broke up, my crew and I left for a three-week shoot in Philadelphia. About a month after I got back from Philadelphia, I tried dating again. This time, I started seeing another woman who was three years older than me. After a few months of dating, she invited me to go to Thailand with her, and since I had spent so much of my life saying "no" to any chance at a romantic adventure, and since I had just had a really intense shoot in Philadelphia, I chose to journey with her to Thailand.

She was studying to be a yoga instructor, she had a soft voice, and seemed really sweet. She too had experienced a traumatic and abusive childhood. Once we got to Thailand, she quickly became emotionally and verbally abusive, and again, I found myself in a situation where I had missed red flags and chosen a partner who was abusive, only this time, I was in a foreign country and even more vulnerable.

On our trip she said things like, "You're spoilt; you're selfish. You love talking about yourself so much. Why don't you make a movie about it?" She would violently ridicule how I dressed, how I navigated, what I ate, and how much or how little I ate. No matter what I did, she found an excuse to be abusive. Looking back at it all, it's obvious to me that she suffered from borderline personality disorder. It was in Thailand that I learnt something incredibly important about myself: In these two relationships I had chosen to spend my time with women who were treating me the way four-year-old Sasha thought that he deserved to be treated.

Once I was reconnected with the scared child inside me, I no longer needed to surround myself with abusive people who behaved like scared four-year-old children. Spiritually, in ignoring, negatively judging and repressing my four-year-old self, I was manifesting painful experiences that would help me become aware of and bring me closer to that part of myself that I was ignoring.

Clearly, even though I had made an increasingly brave choice to share my story with the world and embrace my vulnerability, and even though I was finally allowing myself to be intimate with women, there was still more that I had to work on inside myself. I was still inviting negative people into my life, despite now having many healthy friendships and business relationships. In front of me, I could see a fork in the road. There were signs of a healthy life where I was truly honoring my voice, my needs, my boundaries and the scared child inside of me. But there were also signs that pointed to my past of self-loathing, and feelings of worthlessness and being unloved. I had to make a choice.

SPEAKING MY TRUTH

I cut myself off from relationships that were not healthy for me and this decision has re-energised and revitalised my life. I realised that in order to choose healthy relationships, I had to have a very healthy relationship with myself, and that included loving my inner child.

There's so much more clarity and beauty in my life when I accept, embrace and love myself. While I can't change the past, and I can't control what happens around me, I can choose how I show up in the present moment of my life.

The way I treat myself, the way I treat people around me, the boundaries I choose to set – that's really all I can control.

And in making a concerted effort, in investing energy daily to nurturing and loving myself, I no longer am a prisoner to the needs, expectations and judgements of others, and that's liberating because it allows me to speak to my truth.

But I'm in no way saying that I'm fully healed. What I'm saying is that by choosing to take this journey of looking back at my childhood and sharing it with the world, I've learnt that healing is a journey, not a destination. Healing something inside of myself is a beautiful experience and provides me with the opportunity to gain even more self-awareness and learn about other pieces inside of myself that could benefit from further healing.

As I'm starting to own my voice more and more and starting to respect myself more and more, I've realised there is raw power in being brutally honest with myself and those around me. I'm not going to please everyone. And in exchange for being a people pleaser, in exchange for a zero-conflict experience, I get to have more meaningful relationships and experiences that enable me to continue to grow and evolve as a human being.

THE TEDx TALK

Shortly after I broke off with that woman who had treated me so poorly in Thailand, I started working on my TED talk. I put all of my being into it. I was hungry, I was tired, I was emotionally drained, but I felt more alive and more present than I've ever felt before in my life, and that's how I was when I took the stage at TEDxBozeman. All those experiences over the course of *Rewind To Fast-Forward*, when juxtaposed against my childhood years, gave me a platform to have a public conversation with myself.

What I said on stage completely reflected what I was going through in my life. I learnt so much in the process of making my film. Clearly, I was more self-aware and emotionally present than I had ever been in my life. I spent a lot of years hovering at the edge of my comfort zone and somewhat paralysed by my fears, but in facing what scares me the most and pushing past my comfort zones, I really feel like I continue to give myself every opportunity to heal and to move forward in my life.

REWIND TO FAST-FORWARD

Today, I'm in a healthy, loving, supportive and deeply joyful relationship of two years. She is respectful, nurturing, self-aware, present and kind. I would not have been able to engage in this quality relationship had I not chosen to look inward and take responsibility for my part in choosing unhealthy partners in the past. By taking responsibility for my own wounds, I was able to address them, work on healing them, and in doing so, found deeper self-love. I am now in a relationship with a woman who reflects the self-love and respect I now have for myself.

In August 2016, I had the opportunity to deliver a keynote speech at the Crimes Against Children Conference in Dallas, Texas, where I spoke to 4,200 men and women from law enforcement, social services, Child Advocacy Centers, and various medical practices from all 50 states and 28 other countries from around the world. The success from that conference has led to a public speaking career though my company, Voice For The Kids, LLC (www.voiceforthekids.com). *Rewind To Fast-Forward* is in post-production and we plan to release it in 2018.

In owning my voice, facing my fears, and taking some ownership of the experiences in life, I have given myself every opportunity to grow and heal, while creating a platform from which to use my story as a strong and positive force in the fight against child sexual abuse.

Rewind To Fast-Forward, will help future generations of children, their families, and adult survivors alike. However, with *Rewind to Fast-Forward,* I hope to transcend the boundary between survivors and non-survivors, to engage the world in a global conversation, and to inspire growth, healing, self-awareness, and most importantly, self-love.

2

THU THU

Now in her mid-thirties, Thu Thu was born and raised in Myanmar. She moved to the US in her youth for her studies and returned to Myanmar recently to run an enterprise, which she hopes will be successful. She's also hoping the past stays where it is, even though she had returned to the very place she tried to run away from. She is in a relationship.

....

Coffee Circle, Yangon, Myanmar
25th April 2015

The first time it happened – I was maybe six or seven. I was in Cairo. He was my father's colleague's son. He was probably much older, in his late teens. We were just fooling around. There was no penetration. He was feeling me up, telling me to feel him.

But I noticed that he wouldn't do the same thing to his own sister. I realised that there was something weird going on, not normal. I was quiet but a more "physical" kind of kid. I would punch somebody rather than talk it out. I remember I was always frustrated. I never had the verbal, articulate skills I have now.

THE BEGINNING

When I was 10, I returned to Myanmar, to Yangon.

How did it start? My aunt lives next door. She said to my cousin, her son, "Thu Thu speaks great English." So she suggested to me, why don't you teach your cousin? I had studied in a convent school. My grammar was somewhat solid. He was in class eight or nine.

I still remember the first day. I walked into his room. "Why don't you teach me how to write?" he said.

"Where's your pen?"

He pointed to his penis. "That's the pen we are going to use."

This was literally one to two days after my return from Cairo. It had to be mid-November of that year.

It went from there, building up to penetration. I must have been going to his room from when I was 10 to 11 years old. I got my period when I turned 12. I kept trying to teach him English because I thought it was a service thing. Even when we were kids, we hung out a lot. It was just him fondling me or telling me to fondle him. We had to do it very sneakily. We could do it when his parents weren't around.

It was bound to happen. He was trying to figure it out. Having porn in the house didn't help. My dad had gone to some training in Europe. I remember him bringing back porn magazines and lots of VHS tapes. I used to rummage through the stuff and steal money. And for a while, I started my own business. I did stuff on my own all the time. Lived in my own little world. My neighbours were making tote bags and pencil cases, so I took them to school and sold them. At first, they were giving me commission, and then I figured I could set the prices. That's when I started making really good margins. I literally had no inventory cost or money that I needed to invest in. With the money I made there, I bought watercolour stuff. My parents didn't want me to do arts and crafts. So this way, I was able to do what I wanted without taking a dime from them. That year, I even got the "best attendance certificate". And I wasn't even in class most of the time!

I was present in school but I was in the art teacher's office. We were entering my paintings in competitions. Every month, there would be a theme. We'd paint in a very propagandistic way. It was nationalistic and all that – we were painting all these set messages and different scenes, basically. We painted stuff advocating for the eradication of drugs – heroin was a big issue back in the 1990s. Then the scenes of Thingyan (a water festival), or the boat race – we have traditional rowing races every year.

When I don't have tuition – the extra home classes we had to go to – I'd be out of the house playing in the backyard of my neighbours, or visiting some cousin or another. We'd climb trees, trap birds, or bike around the neighbourhood. I was a very active kid. Our house is here, a cousin's house is there, another cousin's house is at the back. I'm used to going to the different houses.

So my cousin tried [penetration] a couple of times. He didn't know what he was doing. I didn't know what I was doing. There's a certain smell, distinct, very strong. If I smell that – that very strong smell – I'd get put off, a very visceral reaction I have to this day. Much later, I realised it was semen. I can't be with men who even remotely smell like that now.

He used a lot of coconut oil to lubricate but it wouldn't go in. Coconut oil was readily available, for women's hair. It supposedly helps you grow your hair, makes it stronger.

The first time, the penis didn't go in that much: the head and maybe just an inch. It just hurt very much. I was like, what the fuck is going on? He looked at me and said, "You're bleeding." He stopped.

We tried again a couple of weeks later. It was fine. We started having sex. He usually was on top or we did doggy style. He even tried getting into my ass. I don't remember if he did it. Maybe once or twice.

But my cousin wasn't the only person. There was this other guy who tried to fondle me, too. He lived on another street, was older than my cousin, I think. He tried to touch me, my breasts. Tried to get me to suck his dick. I was 11 and a half years old – I was really confused with all these older kids trying all this stuff with me.

Looking back, I wish I was more vocal – had someone to talk to. But I had no one. My little world was spiralling and crashing down when I realised what was happening.

PERIOD

My little world came crashing down badly when I first got my period, right before my 12th birthday. It was the first time my mom spoke to me about "women's stuff". She told me why we have periods, and where babies came from. I was so scared I'd get pregnant.

I finally realised what I had been doing with my cousin was so wrong, and really dirty. I wanted to die right then and there. I started getting depressed and didn't really want to do things. It's probably my hormones getting all crazy, too. But realising I've done such a sick thing on my own accord was the most horrible feeling I had.

I'd go up to my room, which was then on the mezzanine floor, and cry for hours. Then I'd pray. I prayed to be struck by lightning, for God to just end my life right then and there. I was so ashamed of myself. I didn't want my parents to get into trouble. I seriously feared that if I were to have a kid, I would shame my family.

I didn't care what happened to me. I think that was why I still kept quiet even when I knew something very wrong had happened. One time in my sadness, I found my Barbie doll. Her yellow dress had dry cum all over because we didn't have stuff to wipe things with on the mezzanine floor. It stank of semen. I think that was when I really, really wanted to die and disappear.

I cried a lot and prayed a lot: "Take me out of this world." There was no one to tell me it wasn't my fault.

Being pregnant was the thing that freaked me out. I didn't want any evidence. That would mean my family having a bad reputation. That was another source of pressure, growing up. You're taught that you're representing your country and your relationship. Everyone's on the outside, and we were in the group, on the inside.

I told myself that I needed to stop all of this as it's going to be a mess. I realised there was a lot at stake. A switch went on in my head – I became a mature person. My reputation's at stake. I cannot afford to horse around.

I remember feeling very chaotic, and trying to come to terms with myself.

We are Baptists, which is what saved me. When you're 12 and confused, you put your faith in Christ. That was my way out too, to cleanse myself. My little brain told me that things will be OK if I just cleansed myself with holy water. Confess my sins, and become a "child of God". That was the way I thought I had made things right.

So it was a good thing when my family had to leave again when I was 13 and a half.

I kept on meeting him right before though, and he kept on insisting that we do whatever. But I broke it off. It was on one particular day when it all sunk in. A lot of things were going through my head. The first thing, the physical aspect. The second thing, living with myself. The third thing, the shame. The fourth, getting enough courage to say "no, no more". That was the easy part – I had always stood up to him. When we were kids, when I was like two or three years old, he was always teasing me. I'd bite him back or punch him.

I told him that this had to stop. "If you don't stop bothering me, I'd tell your mom about it. Then both our families will be in trouble." His father and my dad were brothers.

That was it, almost like a clean cut. I was 12.

I turned 13 and got baptised. That summer, we had Bible camp. I was in 7th grade. School reopened in June or July. By August, I was out of the country. I was in the United States. The US was a whole entire new world.

HEALING

One was the confrontation, having enough courage to say stop and walk away from it. My coping mechanism was becoming a Christian. I underwent training to be baptised. The whole Christian thing is to be baptised in water and accept Christ. When you immerse yourself in water, you die, and you rise again. I used it as a coping mechanism. So I was able to stand up to the person [my cousin]. But the pressure stayed. Even though I wasn't able to articulate it, my life changed.

When I went to New York, I studied in the eighth grade. From ninth grade onwards, I decided never to go back. I did everything so that my parents could leave me there: Student Council activities, extracurricular activities. I played football et cetera. I remember not being able to sleep at night; I would paint. I wanted very much to improve my English. I kept a journal. I wrote sappy poems which I associated with being a teenager. I loved Ecclesiastes and Socrates and Jiddu Krishnamurti, especially the latter's treatise "On Education". I agreed with Krishna's philosophy, and I recognised why I didn't do so well with rote-learning stuff. That's why I chose to stay in New York. I really wanted to teach. It was nice even though it was depressing. It has helped me tremendously. I'm articulate now and some of my clients would call me a "wordsmith". I could come up with the right words.

But I didn't know why I was crying all the time. I thought of suicide – pills, maybe slit my wrists. But it was my dad's job which held me back. My family, they would get into trouble. That would be very selfish.

So I approached my teacher, Vinnie. I was really lucky that I could do that. Then I met my boyfriend, Chris. I felt that I had a new lease of life. Chris was very open. It took me a long time to talk about my past. He introduced me to Nia, who ran a grassroots NGO that taught people how to write and make films. She was also producing an indie feature film based on her child sexual abuse experience. She was the first person I was able to have a proper conversation with about what had happened to me.

In a sense, my healing was a journey. The baptism was a triage I performed on myself emotionally just to survive and go through the pain. I did whatever I had to. This is why I'm always amazed at the human spirit and how people could bounce back. With Chris and Nia, I could share my feelings and experiences for the first time.

CRASHING

One day, I just disappeared. Stopped taking calls. Dropped off the face of the earth.

By this time, I had effectively cut myself off from the Burmese community and the church. I didn't want to go anywhere or do anything. I would not come out of the house for an entire month. The only reason I would eat was because Chris would get me food.

Before the crash, I also did some speaking engagements, as a young film-maker. At these conferences, I would meet Charles. I don't remember the time I slept with him. I don't remember whether it was before or after the first big depression. I call it "the big depression" because I didn't get out of the house. It was building up all along. I never realised what depression could do to you. I really sunk to the bottom.

To this day, I'm afraid that I'd do it again. That I'd cut the world off and retreat into my shell.

If you're depressed, you really don't want to be depressed. This is what I like about cognitive behavioural therapy (CBT). My partner would tell me, "This is bullshit. You need to stop this in your head, darling."

I know to stop now whenever there are dark thoughts. When the spiral starts happening, I'd take deep breaths, and count, then talk myself out of it. It's amazing how I am now able to talk people out of it when they're spiralling down into depression or panic.

I don't know why it's always women I know who have been depressed, and it's women who have given me good advice. At the back of my mind, it's always been that I get depressed partially because of the stuff that's happened to me.

People say third culture kids[1] are prone to depression. This is what I didn't like; it's not that I didn't get depressed anymore. I didn't want it to be this debilitating thing in my life. I saw that one month just go away.

I started to come out of it – it was really Chris who pushed me to come out of it. If it was not for him, I would probably have killed myself. You really feel that it's really dark – that you're at the bottom of the sea, and you're in this box and you don't have the keys to get out.

I got worried about my depression all the time. Maybe that's why I'm so driven because I refuse to be depressed. Because depression just wastes your time.

---

1   Third culture kids is a term coined by US sociologist Ruth Hill Useem to refer to children who spend their formative years in places that are not their parents' homeland.

CRYING

I couldn't cry.

I used to be yelled at by my dad all the time. He used to be angry. He'd say, "Stop crying at the dinner table!" I hated being yelled at. I still do. It really shocks me and makes me sob when someone I love yells at me. But I understand now that he was stressed out [at work] with all the political shit that was happening.

Now I only cry when pets die. I have stopped crying when people die. When it comes to cats and dogs, I'd start crying. I've learnt not to cry about most things.

GRACE AND HEALING

As soon as my current partner and I started hanging out, I learnt about her dog, Grace. She was abused; she was a rescued greyhound. Greyhounds, especially if they were in the races, were not treated very well. There have been stories of people cutting off the dogs' ears, and then cutting them up and disposing of them. If the dogs had gotten injured, they'd get shot immediately. They are not even considered pets, but livestock in the US. They have tattoos in their ears – one with a serial number and the other with its date of birth. They do that so that people don't switch dogs at the races. So we always knew Grace's birth date!

Grace had a lot of issues. She had abandonment issues. You could not leave her by herself in that house. There's the happiness pee, and the I'm-so-scared-I'm-gonna-pee pee. She'll pee when she's happy to see you. She's peeing all the time!

I recognised the fact that Grace was also a survivor. It was very weird in the beginning: I was at my then boss's place, after dinner, just hanging out, sitting and talking, when she came, sat next to me and put her chin on my lap. She had a brindle type of coat. It's like greyish with spots, black spots. She would shake and her teeth would chatter. When she got stressed out, her body temperature would jump five to ten degrees. They have really long snouts, right? She wouldn't bite, regardless. She was really stupid; she'd sometimes bump into walls. You'd have to be careful, like when she started chasing things without looking at the traffic. She always had to be on a leash. Greyhounds, they are programmed that way. When they see something, they'd just go after it without thinking.

I don't remember when I realised that Grace was helping me. I started learning that dogs can be therapists. My partner told me that she took Grace to the Veteran Association Hospital but first, she had to be trained as a therapist dog. Soldiers also suffer from trauma, post-traumatic stress disorder, but when they pet dogs, the trauma does come out.

For me, it was a different kind of healing. It was not like my partner and I talked. Usually, I'd tell people about my abuse on the first date. When I sensed it was going that way with her, I told her right away. Her son has attention deficit hyperactivity disorder (ADHD). She used to work in a home for autistic children so she understands mental illness.

So my partner started telling me about CBT; she has gone in and out of therapy. She used to think that she was bipolar; now she thinks that she has something else. We found that we were able to understand each other's issues and help cope whenever we're pushed to the deep end by whatever triggers. I guess that's why we became really good life partners.

TRIGGERS

I've been thinking that that was the point when I was "healed" completely. Now I have a coping mechanism, especially with CBT. I know my trigger points: stress and depression. Depression can be accompanied by stress. Depression comes when I'm not meeting my goals. You have the once-in-a-while hormonal imbalance. If I don't have goals or start not believing in the things that I'm doing, then I'll get depressed. And after that… it's just a snowball effect.

Now I've learnt to be a lot more positive. Whenever I think of a negative side of a situation, I'll start thinking about the positive side as well. I don't let myself be sad for a long time because one of the biggest fears that I had coming back home was that I'll be depressed and that I'll fail in the things that I've set out to do, which was to set up this company. That was my biggest fear.

RETURNING

From my room, I can see my aunt's roof; I can see her window. Their home is on the mezzanine floor with Venetian windows with slats. You see, that's where things happened. That was the first thing I looked at when I came back.

My parents had reworked the place for me. I don't have the social support network and the industry contacts, unlike the last city I was living in. People there knew who I was.

Here, I am a nobody. And integrating back into my family, that social pressure is there, especially from my father's brothers and sisters. They're always comparing, at church too, their kids – we have a very successful family – business and careers and all that. We were always comparing about cars and what have you.

I had this huge fear that I would fail as soon as I came back. All those years, I stayed abroad – 20 years. First, it was accidental but then I started ensuring I stayed because I feared that if I came back, I'd actually fall into depression and kill myself. Especially with all the family and societal pressure I'd face.

My family was the first to have a TV, and my relatives would come. They've seen my huge car. My aunt was like, "Are you sure that's your car? That's not your brother's car?" Because I've just returned. Whereas my brother worked his way up. He's talked to his cousins. They know that he's doing something important.

That sort of pressure was there. And starting a business in itself was a daunting task. For me, this is a major time. I want to build a strong foundation so that my girlfriend can join me. I don't want to fall into depression now because then I could still fail. It's like dominos, right? Once it starts falling, you don't know how to stop it.

I don't think I'll fail because of depression – that's what I keep telling myself. Life's been just so darn good, that I'm waiting for the other shoe to drop, the demons to wake again. It's not traumatic anymore but there's always a dark shadow that follows you.

IT CAN HAPPEN TO ANYONE

The biggest challenge I faced was my own demons. I'm still prone to depression, and I still fear getting sucked into the dark place: the place where I'd stop answering emails and phone calls. Where I'd not be able to recover. There are days that I can't get out of bed but I keep thinking about the future that I want to build.

I also feel very privileged. My family had always been in good standing in society. We've always been very devout. We always fit in. I was gifted enough to be "high functioning".

But all that doesn't mean anything when a kid can't speak out to get help. Success isn't an easy thing for girls under normal circumstances in the world. It's even tougher when you've been through abuse.

That's why you have to survive. That's why we have to keep on surviving and tell others that it can happen to anyone.

3

JOHANNES

59-year-old Johannes is a school principal based in North Rhine Westphalia, Germany. He was abused by his maternal grandmother as a child, having grown up in an orphanage after being taken away from his underaged mother. His mother was raped by her father and the latter went to prison as a consequence. Johannes suffered beatings at the hand of his stepfather. As a teenager, he was repeatedly raped by two members of the clergy. He is now married with children and has had a successful entrepreneurial career.

....

a letter
13th March 2016

Dear Eirliani,

I got to know about #FullStop, your campaign to end child sexual abuse, through a Facebook post by Anoushka Shankar[1] in 2015. At that time I was a software architect, and in one of my projects, I had to integrate Facebook into a mobile application. This is how I got a Facebook account.

---

1 Anoushka Shankar is a sitar player and composer.

Being Anoushka Shankar's biggest German fan, I followed her Facebook page immediately.

When I visited your Fullstop website, this video of a young boy in the car of his mother on his way to a soccer training class shocked me. This boy was quiet. He knew what he had to expect from his soccer coach: to be raped. This boy could not talk to his mother.

I felt for him. This boy could have been me.

This movie expressed my own feelings which I still have when I think of my mother. I wish I could hold her in my arms and cry together with her. Cry, because she and I share a terrible time which started in 1956.

BIRTHDAY

On 29th February 1956, my mother turned 16. She must have been a very happy girl that day, because she was allowed to invite her new boyfriend to a small birthday party at her family's house. Her father had returned from war captivity.

My mother, her parents, and her boyfriend celebrated her birthday. It was definitely a special birthday in every sense of the word. It was her fourth real birthday, and her first birthday with her father and her new boyfriend.

February 1956 was the coldest ever February we had in the Sauerland region, which is in the south eastern part of the state of North Rhine Westphalia, a mountainous area in Germany. People in Germany were still suffering from the effects of World War II. Many men had died in war and in prison.

My mother's boyfriend also lost his father in World War II. His father never returned from a mission in Lithuania.

One of his fellow soldiers delivered this message to his mother. This fellow soldier stayed with his mother and he became the stepfather of my mother's boyfriend, who hated him because he treated him terribly. This is what you often hear from stepfathers and stepmothers – that they treated their stepchildren like dogs.

However, the boyfriend was a good catch. Every girl in her town liked him. He was very smart. He always had money to buy drinks for his friends. He was good-looking. He was very handy about mechanical things. And he made some money as a photographer. He was only two or three years older than my mother.

I can just imagine how happy her boyfriend – my natural father – was when he walked the long road to my mother's house.

The house was on the outskirts of this little Sauerland town. It took my father at least one hour to walk the five kilometres from his house to my mother's house. It had been ice cold for days, and it was dark. The way led along a river and a railway track. He had to pass the huge new factory on the left which they built right after the war, with big smoking chimneys.

Behind the factory were two huge rocks known as *Pater und Nonne* ("Padre and Nun" in German). I think my love for rock climbing is somehow related to those rocks. On the way to my mother's house, my father had to pass the huge limestone quarry. I remember that many big trucks with huge rocks passed that way – but at this time of the day, nobody was on the street, except for my father whose heart must have been beating with excitement.

My mother's house was the only residential building in this area. In the house were three flats. My mother lived with her parents on the third floor – right under the roof. There was my mother's bedroom, the bedroom of my grandparents, a kitchen with an oven and with a big table. From the kitchen you could go into the small living room. In the stairwell was a toilet. There was no bathroom. Only very few houses had bathrooms at that time.

I only know from my natural father what happened that very special evening. Everyone had alcohol. The atmosphere was relaxing. At some point, my grandfather started to grope my mother. He undressed her and he even had sexual intercourse with her. He raped her in front of my father – her new boyfriend – and in front of her mother. My father never experienced something like that before. He admitted to me that he was sexually excited and he could not resist when my grandfather talked him into having sex with my mother in front of her parents.

When I heard this story, I wondered why my grandmother did not protect her daughter from her father. She did not. I can only try to understand all this when I think about what people experienced during the war. These terrible experiences must have destroyed their last human feelings. They just tried to forget the war, while the traumatic experiences of the war must have turned humans into heartless machines.

I'm not sure how this evening ended. My father never told me how he felt when he left my mother's house. I am sure he was confused and that he did not foresee the scope of the tragedy he and my mother became a part of.

PREGNANT

My mother became pregnant at the age of 16. She continued dating my father until one evening when he came to my mother's house and my mother was screaming for help from the toilet window. My father saw the blood on the stairs in front of the entry. He believed that this blood was from my mother and that she must have been waiting for him on the staircase after my grandfather tried to induce an abortion with a long needle. My mother was afraid for her life; she was bleeding.

My mother cried and screamed, and she asked my father to run to the priest and ask him for help. Her father wanted to kill the child in her. My father turned around and ran all the way back to the house of this priest. The priest did not ask for further details and he immediately alerted the youth welfare office. And the youth welfare office called the police.

In the 1950s, it was normal that they imprisoned my grandparents and that they sent my mother to a home for so-called "fallen girls". From that day on, my mother was alone, and she was pregnant.

She hated my father because he had informed the priest who in turn had informed the youth welfare officer and because the youth welfare officer had called the police. The police took my grandparents to jail and my mother to a youth home.

I am sure my mother must have felt guilty for what happened to her parents. She must have thought that it was her fault that her parents had to go to prison while she and her boyfriend had fun on her special birthday party.

My mother was allowed to finish school although she was pregnant and lived in a youth home. This was not normal at the time. Usually, they put the youngsters in a youth home where they had to work in the kitchen, in the garden, or do the laundry. I am sure my mother must have made good friends with these nuns. And I can well imagine that this priest played an important role in her life over the next several years.

EARLY YEARS

I was born nine months after this birthday. It was November 1956. My mother was taken to a home run by Roman Catholic nuns 100 kilometres to the west of her hometown. I don't know how long she was in this home. Right after I was born, my mother returned with me to her hometown where she delivered me to an orphanage, while she lived in a home for future paediatric nurses. Both institutions – the orphanage and this nursing school – were run by the same Roman Catholic nurses.

My mother told me that she was not allowed to breastfeed me. She had to deliver the milk at the door of the orphanage in a bottle every day. I can only guess that these Christians nuns were afraid that I would develop a close relationship with my mother, while it was not certain if I would stay with my mother or if another family would adopt me.

I don't remember one single day in the orphanage and I don't even know how many years I stayed there. My father told me that I must have stayed there until my mother turned 21 and until she got married, while my mother keeps telling me that I must have been there for about three years. But she is not sure.

I only know from my mother that I almost died at the age of three when the intestine intertwined with my stomach. I was extremely skinny so that the thin layer between the stomach and the intestine broke or even vanished. This is a dangerous situation, because nothing could go in and out of your body while you develop the most dangerous infections. I was lucky that the nurses understood that my crying and screaming was not normal that day. My mother said they rescued my life at the very last minute, but they did not give permission for my mother to attend the surgery.

A few days later, the surgery scar opened because I was crying and screaming so much, and they had to save my life a second time.

When I see small children of the age of three, I can imagine how much I must have been crying for love from my mother. But my mother was not allowed to be with me. She had to care for herself. She had no power to protect me, to love me, and to care for herself. Like how her own mother had no power to protect her from her own father when he raped her in front of her mother.

My mother got married in November 1962 to a man who also came from a terrible family. His natural father had had an affair with a girl. The girl became pregnant, and so his father asked his brother to marry this girl and care for the child as if it was his own. It was in the days leading up to the war. The war atmosphere breeds the craziest creatures.

It was terrible. You can just imagine that the husband of my mother was not a child of love. No – definitely not. And my mother sometimes said that she married this guy because nobody else wanted a girl with a child.

Honestly, whenever she said this to me, I wondered why she cared about me. She could have left me at this orphanage, hoping that someone would adopt me. Actually, the parents of my natural father wanted to adopt me. But my mother hated my father, and she did everything – everything! – to ensure he could not get in touch with me.

My mother married her new love on the day of her father's birthday. Yes – it is true. She got married on the birthday of the man who raped her six years earlier. She got married on the birthday of the man who ruined the lives of her and my natural father. I will never understand why she did this.

Right after she got married, my last name was changed to the name of her husband's, although this man never adopted me. I'm not sure why she did not want me to be adopted by her new husband. Changing the family name to the name of a person whom you are not even related to was, and still is, illegal. My mother must have had good friends who helped her, and I believe that it was this priest.

Nobody should know my real identity. Not even I should know. Today I know that everyone in my mother's hometown knows my story.

LEAVING THE ORPHANAGE

After they got me out of the orphanage, I spent some time at the house of my grandparents. Isn't it crazy that a mother who had been raped by her father takes her five- or six-year-old child to the house of her parents so that they'd look after this child? Whenever I shared this situation with friends or with a psychotherapist, these people were shocked. It took me until I started to share my story with you, Eirliani, that I understood the tragedy of this move of my mother.

I am not sure how long I stayed with my grandparents. This depends on when I was taken out of the orphanage. I just hope that I stayed there for only half a year. There were no other children. I just want to believe that my mother saw how terrible life was at these Roman Catholic orphanages and that she must have thought that everything else was better – even a place without children but with a couple who raped their own daughter. I am sorry to say that: but I still cannot understand how a human being can do something so stupid.

During the daytime at my grandparents', I was alone with my grandmother. My grandfather, my mother and my new stepfather were at work, I think. Funnily enough, I can't recall seeing my mother and my stepfather at this place. It is as if they were never there.

In my photo album, there is a picture where I sleep in my mother's bed. From this I believe that they always took me to bed in my mother's bedroom. But when I woke up, I was usually next to my grandmother and everybody else was away.

My grandmother always pulled me very tight to her body and she would touch me all over. It felt strange somehow, but I let her do it because there was nobody to whom I could turn. And... it felt better than being in the orphanage. What was the alternative for this little child? If I rejected my grandmother or if I were to ask my mother – where was she? – I would have risked being taken back to the orphanage. No!

This is how I learnt that I should never reject a woman.

They could do – and they did – whatever they wanted to do with me. I was always their playboy – a boy to play with.

I remember that in the afternoons, I often sat in the cold kitchen of my grandparents' flat – all naked – on the big old dining table. I'm not sure why I sat there all naked. Is this normal for a child? One day, the door of the kitchen opened and my mother stood in front of me. I was shocked. Where did my mother come from? Nobody had expected her. My mother asked my grandmother what I was doing there. This was when I realised my grandmother was standing right behind me. Where did she come from? Was she always there when I sat naked on the dining table?

She replied to my mother, "There is nothing wrong. He is just discovering his body."

I felt so terribly shy and guilty this very moment. Why was my mother shouting at my grandmother, and what had my grandmother done with me?

MOVING

In spring 1963, I moved to the house of my parents in a different part of my mother's home town, some 10 kilometres away from her parents' house. It was a wonderful place for me. I remember this place in the huge forest on top of a small hill as the most beautiful place I had ever lived in. My parents hated this old farmhouse because the house was old and the ceiling had come down once. There were rats in the house and you had to pass them whenever you wanted to go upstairs to the bedrooms.

My mother told me that it was difficult at that time to find a flat. You had to be married in order to be authorised to rent a flat. All Germany was full of refugees from the former Eastern parts of Germany which were now occupied by Poland and Russia. Many houses were destroyed during the war.

I loved this place in the middle of nowhere. There were children close by. I spent every day outside, from the morning until the evening. We played in the forest, in the fields, on the grass. We played hide-and-seek. We ate the wild fruit from the forest. We played with ants. I had a sheep next door which I named. People in this place kept rabbits and chicken. There was a beekeeper.

The ranger in the forest loved me and took me out from time to time. We had cold winters with lots of snow and we drove the sled all the way down the hill. It was so beautiful. I had so much fun.

However, whenever I did something wrong in the eyes of my mother, she would ask my stepfather to beat me. He then pulled my trousers down, beating me until he was exhausted. I still have this feeling as if this beating would last forever. After being beaten, I could not sit on a chair or lie on a bed. My whole body burnt like fire.

I was scared of my stepfather. I was scared of my mother. I was an undernourished small boy of only six or seven years. Keep in mind that my natural mother asked her husband to beat me. She watched him beating me! How can a mother watch a man beating like hell her own flesh and blood? What have they done to her that she could act like this without feeling guilty? I would kill my partner if she were to touch my child.

There were two trails through the forest leading to our hill.

At the end of one of these paths was a pub. My stepfather was a drinker. Every other day, he and my mother sent me with a big brown leather bag in the darkness all the way down to this pub to buy beer for them. I can't remember how many half litre bottles fit into this big bag – it must have been at least 12. Carrying this bag was not the worst part of the task. The worst part was the fact that my mother and her husband always told me that I should run away if a foreign man comes after me.

All my childhood, my mother and my stepfather were afraid that my natural father or his parents would look for me and that they would try to adopt me. Later, my natural father told me that he and his parents had always wanted to adopt me.

Just imagine being a small child of six or seven or eight years with a big brown bag full of beer bottles. You have to walk through a dark forest all the way down to this pub. On your way back, you have to carry all the full bottles uphill. With every noise, with every movement, you start seeing a foreign man behind every tree. What would you do? I was so scared every time I walked this path in the dark. But I never saw a man coming after me.

MY GRANDMOTHER

When I was 14, I started to live in a kind of dream world like most children do at that age. I stayed in my room as much as I could and I dreamt of being a radio star one day. In the nights, I dreamt of living in Canada as a woodcutter. And I dreamt of living like a Native American in the prairie, going through many wild adventures. My mother and my stepfather had no idea that these wild adventures also involved some wild, sexual dreams. I definitely became a man – not just in my dreams.

I started to read the Bible. I'm not sure why. Was it that I felt that my sexual adventures in my dreams were something bad? I believe so, because looking and touching my own body was, and still is, tightly related to this terrible experience with my grandmother. Nobody was allowed to touch my body. Not even I was allowed to touch it. There were areas of my body which I did not want to touch at all. This feeling is still there. Thank you, grandmother.

In the orphanage, I must have learnt that reading the gospel can clean all sins. Sex was a sin. And reading the Bible compensated for the wildest sexual dreams. This is what I learnt in the orphanage.

I listened to the radio as often as possible and I dreamt of creating my own radio shows. One day, an old artist gave me a tape recorder and I started my first recordings for a comedy show. I submitted tapes with my own sketches to the radio station. They broadcast them from time to time in the most popular radio shows. I could see how my stepfather became proud of me. And this encouraged me to go even further.

I was 14 when my parents often travelled to visit the parents of my stepfather. I was wondering why they only visited his family, but never the parents of my mother. One Sunday afternoon, the phone rang and someone from the family of my mother said that something terrible had happened: they had found the body of my grandmother in the house. I was asked to tell my mother to come to the house of her parents immediately to care for her father. My mother and my stepfather returned some time later. I told them about the phone call, and they immediately drove to the house of my maternal grandparents. Later, they told me that the lifeless body of my grandmother was found in her bedroom. The neighbours smelt something strange in the house and that they had not seen my grandparents for a long time.

Nobody knew exactly when my grandmother died or how she died. My grandfather was found in the same bed next to her. When people entered the room, my grandfather was trying to wake up my grandmother. It was in vain. She was dead. The ambulance took my grandfather to the hospital.

My grandmother was buried in her hometown. My mother hardly ever visited the grave, and I still wonder why. What relationship did she have with her mother? Was my mother angry with my grandmother because she did not help her when she was raped by my grandfather? Was she angry because she saw my grandmother touching my naked body in the kitchen? Or what was it? I wish I could ask my mother.

TAPE RECORDING CLUB

At the age of 14, I founded a tape recording club with members all over Germany. I contacted 14 makers of the comedy show which my stepfather loved to hear, and this guy got me in touch with many others with the same interests. We all created our private comedy shows and publicised them within the circle. The tapes were sent from member to member. It took months until a tape with a show came back to the original sender. Nowadays, we would use modern podcasting using the internet. But at that time, people were patient and we took more time to do things.

One day, the newspaper in our town got to know about my activities with the tape recorder club. I was very proud when they published a big article about me as a 14-year-old club founder. My picture was on the paper, together with my name. I was famous in our city!

A few days later, someone called at our house. He introduced himself as Werner Müller. He and his friend were deacons in the Roman Catholic church and they had a great network in the church. They wanted to meet me because they wanted to help introduce me to the most important people who could make my life successful. My mother and my stepfather gave permission to invite the both of them. They came to our house. Both had the same first name "Werner". Again, they told my mother and me that they could help me with a bright future and that they wanted to introduce me to the most influential people in the church. My mother liked the guys.

I felt a bit strange. They had nothing in mind with regard to my tape recorder club. They were much older than me. Yes – my mother liked them both, and I wanted to please her. Children always want to please their parents.

The two Werners invited me for the weekend to where they worked and where they lived. It was some 25 kilometres away from my parents' house. They picked me up in their car.

The place belonged to the order of the Alexianer. It was a mental hospital run by the monks. These two Werners lived in a beautiful house just next to the hospital together with other male nurses and monks. The whole environment had a mixed atmosphere consisting of clerical and monastic life, and of a mental hospital.

Wherever you looked, you saw monks and mentally ill people. You'd hear the church bells ring every now and then. It was definitely a holy place. And everything that happened here in this place was good – I was sure that it was good, because I still believed that whatever clerical people do was good. I was sure that my mother was proud of me now that these high-ranking people from the church had contacted us and introduced me to a secret Christian network. I was sure that whatever happened here would be good, and that it was the will of God and of my mother that I was here.

The two Werners showed me around. How would a 14 or 15-year-old boy feel in this environment? I definitely felt uncomfortable. No doubt about it. But at the same time, I felt extremely proud that I was introduced to this secret world that none of my friends at school would probably ever see in their lives.

In the evening, they took me to their house. They offered me alcohol to drink and they encouraged me to drink a lot. They gave me the feeling that alcohol was good if you wanted to be in this environment. I remember how excited I was when I entered this all-new world.

Their rooms were packed with impressive books and paintings. The rooms were furnished with style. Wow – this was so impressive. They told me about the secret power of the secret philosophical society "Rosicrucianism" and that they could invite me to those secret meetings one day.

The alcohol affected me. I still was not used to alcohol at all, and I did not want my mother and my stepfather to see me drunk. Hence, I agreed to stay with them overnight. They called my mother and told her that I would stay overnight and that I would come back the next day. My mother trusted them.

The first night, these two Werners stayed in the same room as me. When I lay down to sleep, the older one came close to me and started touching my body. I did not want this, but both of them told me that it was alright to have sex at that age and to have sex with men. They told me that it was normal in monasteries and in secret spiritual circles for men to have sex with one another.

I was drunk. There was no way to reach home. I could not call anyone for help. Who would have helped me? Who would have believed me? I don't know how to describe this feeling of having an old, fat man lying at your back, touching your body. Feeling his alcoholic breath at the nape of your neck. Hearing his excited breath right behind you. I felt terrible, but I could not run away. It was a very strange feeling which I had never had before. It was definitely different from how I felt when I had my sexual dreams of being a Native American in my own bed.

Both Werners were in my bed now. Touching me all over and touching me everywhere. They asked me to touch them. Can you imagine how terrible it is for a child to touch the hairy belly of an old man? These guys were at least three to four times older than I was. They were ugly. They wanted me to touch their penises and to rub them. They asked me to kiss their bellies and to swallow their penises.

It was so disgusting. And they kept rubbing my penis. I hated the feeling of being drunk, of being sexually excited. I felt completely disgusted from touching these fat, old, hairy bodies.

At some point, the younger Werner left the room and I had to stay with the older one on my own. He did not give up touching me and to talk me into touching him. I think at some point, I must have given in to completely satisfying him, just so that he would stop using me. He must have fallen asleep at some point and I could move out of his bed.

The next day, I wanted to leave as soon as possible. Both of them said that they had to work and that I should take the bus back home. They explained to me that now I was an adult and that what I experienced the night before was just normal. Everybody in church did this.

I remember how I started to look at the other monks in this monastery and at the other male nurses in this mental hospital. I really thought that it was normal that the clergy, who live under the oath of celibacy, have sex with one another.

I took the bus back home that day and I believe that I must have felt like this boy from your video. I had nobody to talk to about what happened that night with these two clerical men. I did not trust my mother. I just wanted her to be proud of me – proud, because I had these two seemingly very influential deacons with a good network from the most secret inner circles of the Church. I wanted my mother and my stepfather to be proud of me, and not to have problems with me. They had problems with me all their lives. This is the feeling they gave me.

It did not take too long until these two Werners called again and asked me if I wanted to come back. My mother noticed that, and she gave "permission". What would she have thought about me if I had rejected the friendship of these two deacons? I was sure that she would have thought that I did not appreciate what all these people were doing for me.

I don't know how often I gave in to meeting with these two Werners, and how often I satisfied these "holy" men. But it took me a while before I realised that they would definitely not help me when it came to my further education.

I think I was about to finish secondary school and I was looking for the next step. I was hoping that these two Werners would open a new path for me, so that I could get my high school certificate from a Roman Catholic boarding school or something similar. I am not sure which excuses they had for me and why they could not help me. All my hope was in vain.

I was just a cheap call boy for two deacons for about two years. I started to reject their invitations, but I did not tell my mother about it. And they never called at my home again.

MY FATHER

It was my 18th birthday. I had no friends in Germany. No party was planned. On that day, my mother had some other commitments. My stepsister was also not at home. I was alone with my stepfather on that day. I should add that until that day, I was made to believe that my stepfather was my real father.

When I returned home from school, I found a big brown envelope on my desk in my little room. The sender was the youth welfare office. I opened the envelope and I could not believe my eyes: the letter said that with my 18th birthday, the guardianship of the youth welfare office ended. They had included documents from court cases vis-à-vis a man I had never heard of. The documents said that this man was my father.

My mother was not at home. My stepsister was not there. I was waiting for my stepfather to come home from work. It was my 18th birthday – probably the most important day in the life of a youth. Other classmates celebrated their theirs with big parties. And I was alone with a big brown envelope from the youth office. There was nobody to ask if my whole life in this family was just one big lie. My stepfather came back from work. My mother tasked my stepfather to explain everything to me. When I was a small child, my mother tasked my stepfather to beat me to hell. And now on my 18th birthday, she tasked him to explain to me that everything was just a big lie.

My stepfather asked me if I ever had the impression that he was not my real father. And I said, "Yes." I often had the feeling that a real father could not treat his real child like how this man had been treating me. I am not sure how he reacted when I said this to him. But he continued telling me his version of the truth.

He told me that I have my good looks from my mother, and that I do not resemble my natural father at all. He told me that my natural father was a gangster and he had betrayed my mother when he was young. That he left her when she was pregnant with me and that my mother was glad that he – my stepfather – had married her. Otherwise, she would not have found another man and I would have had to stay in the orphanage forever. My stepfather told me that my natural father was not an honest man, and that he ran several companies into bankruptcy. I should stay away from this man, otherwise he would only create bigger problems for me.

I was not able to talk to my mother about all this because I felt that my mother was very sad about this terrible story. And I felt guilty that I had created all these problems for her – that I ruined her youth, that she had to marry this man who treated me so terribly. I pitied my mother and I did not want to give her more problems. I just wanted to leave my family as soon as possible.

I left home the same year – at the age of 18. First, I joined the army for one and a half years, and then I accepted a job in Frankfurt, 300 kilometres away from home.

I worked for an international record company. I was collecting information from record shops all over Germany. I felt lonely in this huge town, and while I was travelling. And I was dreaming of finding a woman. I contacted a marriage agency, and they introduced me to some ladies of the same age. How crazy does this sound nowadays: a youngster of 20 or 21 years who would ask a marriage agency to find them a woman or man? However, one of the girls I met invited me to visit her sister in Munich. She was married to a lawyer. We travelled there and I told them what my stepfather had told me about my natural father.

This lawyer asked me if I had ever validated the story of my stepfather and he suggested that I should try to find my natural father and meet him in person. He told me that I should not believe everything that my parents told me. This was new to me: an adult suggesting that I should not believe my own parents.

The next day, I went to the post office in Munich and looked up the name of my natural father in the telephone directory. I called the number of his company from a phone booth. A lady answered. I introduced myself and I asked for the man with the name I remembered from the youth welfare office documents.

A few seconds later, a man answered the phone. He seemed to be extremely happy to hear my voice. Yes, it was my natural father. No doubt: it was him.

He asked me to visit him as soon as possible. I believe I promised to meet him one or two weeks later. I was so happy that I had spoken to my natural father for the first time.

I drove the 200 kilometres with my car to his house. Everything was different from what my stepfather had told me. I met my father, his wife, two stepsisters and two stepbrothers. I was hoping that I finally found a family who wanted me – a family where I was most welcome.

My stepbrothers and stepsisters and I had so much fun that weekend. They showed me how to ride the motorbike. They took me around and showed me the places which I remembered from my childhood. I felt so good. You wouldn't believe how happy I was.

Unfortunately, the weekend had to come to an end. My father explained to me that his wife had a problem with this situation, because he was still in love with my real mother.

He said that his wife did not want me to return to their house again because she was afraid that my father would leave her. Can you imagine how I felt when I heard all this?

However, my father told me the whole story of what happened when my mother was pregnant with me. He mentioned this priest and he encouraged me to talk to the priest if I wished to validate the whole story.

I did. I found the priest in another village, 50 kilometres to the south of my mother's home town. I called him. He answered the phone, and I introduced myself.

"What do you want?" he asked. I told him that I wanted to find out the truth of my childhood and that I met my natural father a few days ago, and that he had told me a completely different story to what my stepfather had told me. The priest said, "I don't want to talk about it. I was transferred to this place for disciplinary reasons because of you." And he dropped the call.

Again, it was me who created problems for other people: for my mother and my stepfather, for my natural father and his wife, and now even for this priest. Other people were suffering just because of me: of my being in this world.

The same year, I wanted to celebrate Christmas with my mother and my stepfather. I travelled the 300 kilometres with my car over snowy and icy roads to their place. On the first evening, I sat with my mother in the same room. My stepsister, my grandfather, and my stepfather had gone to bed already. I told my mother quietly that I had met my natural father a few months before, and that I like him a lot. That I met my stepbrothers and stepsisters. That he had a beautiful house. That he had shops for bicycles and motorbikes. That he had a good business. I had the impression that my mother was happy to hear this from me. I told her that I will not tell her husband, because I knew that he did not like that.

The next morning, my stepfather asked me to leave the house and to travel back to where I had come from. He did not want to see me anymore because I would ruin his family, with my relationship with my natural father. So I left.

MARRIAGE AGAIN

In 2001, I married my second wife. She and I have a daughter who is 14 by now. My wife is calm, very calm. And she was the first person to give me the feeling that I am OK the way I am.

Well, my wife is not my therapist. I cannot discuss with her my childhood, my time at the orphanage, my parents. It was only two or three weeks ago that I told her about the sexual abuse by these two deacons. She can't help me with these problems, but she accepts at least that I face these problems and that I want to clear them with people I trust. I think my wife is the first person who trusts me – no matter what I do. I never had this feeling with a woman before.

Over the last months, I have learnt a lot.

I have learnt how important it is to face your problems instead of denying them and instead of running away from them. We have the capability to move traumatic experiences to our subconscious, so that they are not always present in our daily life. In a way, it is a perfect way to survive dramatic situations. I don't remember one single day at the orphanage. Nothing.

Today, I know that the memories of these times would have killed me. My body wanted to die when I was three years old. What is left from this event is just a big surgery scar in the abdomen. But once those traumatic experiences are moved to the subconscious, you have no control over them where they tended to develop into neurotic behaviour.

I still have a problem when people come close to me. I can't stand it if a woman wants to hug me – not even my wife can do this. I can't stay in bed in the mornings with a woman next to me – I have to leave the bed. This is why I have my own bedroom now. Otherwise, I would not get enough sleep.

Again, once you move your traumas to your subconscious, you lose control over them. You are not even aware of them, and it is hard and almost impossible to integrate these traumas into your life.

I have learnt that the best therapists are those people who have experienced something similar. I have seen many therapists in my life – but none of them really helped me. It was frustrating – you pay all this money, and nothing helps. Only people who have experienced something similar in their life can respond to your feelings in an authentic way. I still have not found out how it works.

Is it the tone of our language? Is it our body language? Is it our smell? Our taste? Our eyes? I don't know.

Epilogue: a letter
10th August 2017

Writing my story from the perspective of a survivor – of a victim of sexual abuse – took a big burden off my shoulders and opened my eyes to the different aspects of my vita. Actually, after writing this story, I could make peace with myself, with my mother, my stepfather, my grandmother, my grandfather, with these two deacons of the Roman Catholic Church, and with my first wife and children from whom I am separated for some years now. I hope they will get to read the following:

Your personality – your individuality – grows from the relationship with your social environment, from the relationship with your mother, with your father, and with whomsoever is closest to you, especially during the first years of your life. In these first years of our life we only know the "we", and from this "we", we develop the "I". It is the quality of this individual relationship with another person that determines if you will be a strong or a weak person, if the world is good or bad, if you will be in an active or passive state with regard to the world and to the society you are a part of.

In this relationship with other people, we sense their reactions to us. When do others react to us in sympathy and make us feel good, and when are they repulsed and make us feel bad about ourselves?

In my story, I mentioned two events which I would relate to sexual abuse – one was the event when my mother entered the kitchen of my grandmother and saw me naked, and the other was when these two deacons had sex with me.

There is definitely nothing wrong with hugging and caressing someone you love from the bottom of your heart. What made me feel bad was the reaction of my grandmother and my mother when they both gave me the feeling that there was something wrong in being hugged and caressed by my grandmother. Their reaction triggered a paranoia in me and led to trauma from which I suffered for roughly 45 years. My body literately turned into a frozen state whenever a woman hugged and caressed me.

The other event of sexual abuse was that with the two Roman Catholic deacons. One must keep in mind that my upbringing in a Roman Catholic orphanage without parents left me with a weak personality, with this constant feeling of being small and guilty, and with an admiration for church authorities. When these two deacons introduced themselves, they promised me to introduce me to a higher and secret level of our society where I could find security for the rest of my life. How cool was that from the perspective of a teenage boy with a weak personality? I must have taken this as a sign from God.

These deacons were aware of the huge cognitive gap between them and me. They knew that I would admire them like gurus. And they knew that by forcing me into secrecy on everything they showed and did to me, I would regard myself as privileged. Talking about these secret events to others would have meant losing my privileged state and falling back into a guilty and worthless one.

I am pointing this out so clearly, because I believe that the combination of a weak young personality and a self-declared guru is extremely dangerous. From my perspective, this is why we see sexual abuse happening so often between children and relatives, priests, teachers, spiritual gurus, or coaches.

I wish that every child has a mother who can stay close to the child at least for the first two years. And if this is impossible for whatever reason, then this mother should make sure that this child is taken care of by someone she really trusts and by someone with a good personality.

I wish that our societies focus as much on personal relationships as we do on physical resources. If we want to have a strong and healthy society, then for the sake of their children, we must provide families with a social environment where they don't have to fear social and materialistic poverty.

I was more than lucky that in the years after I was 45, two women crossed my way who helped me grow into a strong and happy personality: my second wife and an Indian woman, who showed me the beauty of our nature and of our life. It is really an exception.

And I was happy to meet Lin who listened to my story without any judgement.

4

CLARA

51-year-old Clara of Welsh origins, grew up in Canada and has lived 20 years in Germany. Her father practised the occult. Both parents suffered trauma as children. At 17, Clara became a child prostitute. She was beaten up by a stranger and left for dead. Today, she runs a successful shop together with her partner.

....

Hotel Seehof in Charlottenburg, Berlin
17th May 2015

HIRAETH IS MY SHIP

There's a beautiful word in Welsh: *hiraeth*. H-I-R-A-E-T-H. What it means is "the longing for one's spiritual home". I guess the reason why I've survived is because I'm longing for my spiritual home. Which is here, right now, with you.

It's the truth, sweetie. It's real. Aren't we lucky?

We were Welsh, my father and I. We were Druids. Listeners of the stones, that's what we called ourselves. We listen to the stones speak. There's a song that we sing in Wales, it's so beautiful, it's about *hiraeth*, because our spiritual home is here.

Far away the voice is calling,
Bells on memory chime,
Come home again, come home again,
They call through the oceans of time.

We'll keep the welcome in the hillsides,
We'll keep the welcome in the vales,
This land you love will still be singing,
When you come home again to Wales.
This land you love will keep a welcome and with a love that
never fails,
We'll kiss away each hour of hiraeth till you come home again
to Wales,
We'll kiss away each hour of hiraeth, till you come home again
to Wales.

It's my favourite word. If I have a home one day, I'll call it *hiraeth*. If I have a boat, you know, I'll call it *hiraeth*.

Hiraeth is my ship. *Hiraeth* is my ship.

We're lucky, we are, Lin.

a series of emails
26th January 2015

The symptomatic behaviours of possible perpetrators of sexual abuse as indicated in an article in the weekend newspaper describes aspects of my personality for which I have often been criticised by relatives and in relationships. They fit me to a T. Watch for "professional youths", people who relate to young people as a young person, disregarding generational role differences, it warned. When I read that, my heart leapt a beat.

First of all, I know that victims may become perpetrators. Secondly, although I have never abused any child knowingly in any way, shape or form, the lack of boundaries and clarity in role differentiation has left a lot of grey areas in my relationships, especially those with my own children. This inability to play a proper parental role, the "befriending" of my children created a huge rift between their father and me. It was him against us. This seeming solidarity maintained my victim/martyr status, and damaged my children into adulthood. Other relationships were strained; teachers, school administrators, policies and systems all made me feel admonished for my alliance with my children – I felt my allegiance to them was out of love. I could not understand anything other than Them versus Us.

Reading this article yesterday also relieved me of the guilt and shame – the feeling that I always had to defend myself against the perceived criticism – and eradicated my self-doubt which began to recur as I started facing my abuse ("Maybe I am making a mountain out of a molehill"). It confirmed that there had been something dreadfully wrong with my relationships from a very early age. It assured me that my behaviour was typical for a victim of abuse.

Oddly enough, this grain of information from the paper served to budge something big in me, a boulder which had been firmly lodged between me and my voice. Today I found my voice. I told my partner how I felt when he ignored my presence. I told my son how angry I was at his recent behaviour and I applied consequences for this behaviour. I told these important people in my life how I felt, WITHOUT making them feel wrong. I was honest about my infringed-upon boundaries.

It felt so good to have my voice for the first time. I cried tears of joy, tears of victory, tears of gratitude.

I am walking free. Free. The prison of victimhood has dissolved.

27th January 2015

My potty was blue. Light blue plastic, the same colour as the plastic fish with the big, friendly, black eyes I used to bathe with as a child. Inoffensive, clean, neutral, innocent.

I remember nothing in particular; dissociation is like that. But I do remember who managed the potty and the emptying of its contents. It was not me.

I brought it with me when I moved to Berlin. My aunt had kept it over the years like a sacred object. My blue potty.

My mother used to recount the story of me "doing a number" beneath the stairs. Was this a kind of protest towards that clean blue potty? Or was it a backlash at the Aunty who I know made me feel horribly ashamed for being a dirty girl?

Where was the dirt? Where was the girl?

Why didn't she keep the friendly fish instead of the gaping blue sky on which I was to become "clean"?

How was a dirty girl like me to be kept clean?

I can't remember.

2nd February 2015

Much love and VERY excited to see you and SHARE! The Moon is between us always, she is our friend.

I wrote a lullaby for my nephew and sang it to all of the children as they came by, one by one...

Verse 1

The moon is your friend
She's always there for you
You know just what She wants you to do,
The Moon is your friend
She's up in the sky tonight
(Can you see her)
Repeat Verse 1.
(Can you hear her)
Repeat Verse 1.
(Can you feel her).
Yes Princess,
We have been connected forever through her sylvan ways.
May the Force be with you.

4th February 2015

Perhaps there is a reason she cannot bear talking to me at depth or for any longer than a few minutes. She told me once she did not like me. She said I was far more fun when I was drinking. She said I was like my father. Maybe I reminded her of her mother, whom she openly hated.

In my adult life, I have called for my Mama twice. Both times of excruciating pain, experiencing emotional memories of sexual abuse buried by years of dissociation and alcohol abuse. At these moments, when this live-or-die pain gripped me and shook my foundation, I called for Mama. I had never referred to her as Mama at all. I called her Mum or Mummy, but never Mama. Yet in these two moments, she became Mama.

Of course, I was alone. The anguish of that aloneness which brought me to God. Was God my Mama perhaps? Or was Mama God? Both seem correct. So who was Mummy, or Mum? The woman who answered my long-distance calls with, "What do you want – quickly – I'm going out."

Could I have been crying for this seeming stranger? Or was my soul crying out to hers, through whose body I was created? Whose pain did I remind her of? Perhaps there is a reason she does not like talking to me at depth. I no longer take it personally.

I know what Mama is. It's a feeling, a vast surrender, an empty scream in the gaping crevice of a broken heart.

It is where I found myself.

5th February 2015

I would have named you Laila. In October this year, 2015, you would have turned 18.

You have never left me, I know you have always stayed close. Now I will let you speak – you have surely got so much to tell me, and in October, we will celebrate well.

I will make it up to you.

Love, Mama.

15th February 2015

I am dreaming. Or is it real? Confusion. Terror. Pleasure. I am enjoying this. Am I? Tingling all over my body. Who is that? I can't see. Only feeling. Hands probing, touching. Who are you? (Who is he?) No sound from my mouth. Somewhere, someone is crying – whimpering- is that me? (Who is that?) No, I was just moaning with pleasure. Or was I? Do little girls of 10 years old moan out of sexual pleasure? Am I 10 or am I 49? I am petrified, cannot move. Frozen, I lie in bed and dream. I am dreaming now (am I?). I am 49 years old. (Am I?). I am alone, all alone. (Am I?)

My friend has just broken up with me again… he says I am obsessed with him. (Am I?) Please protect me – don't leave me alone, I am frightened to be alone… My girlfriends cannot help me. They are busy… or are they afraid of me too? They don't call back. (Please help me!)

I wake. It is 4.30am and he is there in my bed with me. Touching me. Feeling my body gently. Tingling sensations… please don't touch me there (it feels so good). I don't know who you are and why you are in my bed. Who is crying in the hallway? It is my girlfriend who stayed overnight. Then. Not now. She is real. (Was real.)

I am dreaming. I am 49. I am alone. Completely alone in this memory of my bed, which like a lost vessel, floats aimlessly on a boundless ocean. I want to die. I cannot do this alone. Oh God please help me. Please. I do not want to drink. I do not want to kill myself. Give me strength and steer my boat (my bed) home to a safe and sunlit shore.

I lie alone in bed and cry endless tears. Why can I not keep this forgotten? Why is he in bed with me still?

I am alone.

I am 49.

It is over now.

I sleep again and wake to my 7.30 alarm clock. Clock, it is a clock.

17th February 2015

Now that my partner told me he wants nothing to do with me outside of business, and has told me that my problems are a real turn-off for him, I am starting to feel rage.

I am raging at the man who got in my bed with me when I was little. I have no idea how on earth I should or can forgive him. I thought I had… I was wrong. As I see this breakdown of my relationship as a result of my childhood abuse, I feel murderous. Have you experienced this? Is this perhaps universal now? I cannot understand the psychology of it. Have you some recommended reading?

The idea of having to spend time with someone who is abandoning me in my time of need is like reliving the original incident. I have no clue what to do. Part of me wants to stop this writing and let it be… Because I have no chance to escape and process. I have to work every day, and in business with a man who is pulling away from me every step I come closer to the pain.

What is your feeling? Do you have any suggestions for me? I feel horribly endangered right now…

Much love and hope that this is going to be alright.

20th February 2015

I was dreaming again… I looked down at my straw sandals and saw that I was leaving bloody footprints, then realised that my pants were soaked thoroughly with fresh, red blood. I was in the shop talking with customers and could not just walk away without leaving bloodied footprints. At that moment of intense discomfort and awareness that at any moment the blood could overflow the fabric, my partner walked in. He took over talking to the customers and I could run to privacy. I woke up feeling released of the physical trauma memory and cleansed. At yoga that same morning, my teacher Martina intuitively worked with the hips and gall bladder. I feel relieved of the memory of that horrible fear cramp.

I also feel freed from the need to have my partner understand. For now. I realise he is dealing with his own abuse. Or not…

Sleep well, dearest Lin, and may Goodness bless you on your journey home.

10th March 2015

Unfortunately we alcoholics are accustomed to people dying on us in various ways… they drink, they commit suicide, they die of cancer… I must admit it is the first murder I have ever experienced, but I got over the drama quickly after the initial shock.

I went with my former partner to put flowers outside her house and to say a prayer. He helped me, in a way, by just moving on. He has seen lots of horrible things as a former law enforcement officer. I find enormous strength by keeping the focus on myself and in a corner of my heart, I believe that he is actually helping me by forcing me to focus on myself. I am very good at living life through someone else, and keeping my light to myself.

Hope springs eternal in the human heart and I feel that he is my partner, no matter what. Of course my world will shatter if he comes along with a new partner after telling me he is not capable of having a relationship.

I also have learnt in my recovery to stay in the day. That is what I do. These sorts of things always usually lead an alcoholic like myself back to the bottle. For this reason, I must talk about this sneaky disease and its solution… and all of the disease's ramifications constantly with fellow sufferers who need guidance, lest I forget it is waiting to get me.

That is the way it is for someone recovering from alcoholic, spiritual AND sexual abuse. Constant vigilance through never-ending thought of others. I sometimes feel like a special agent of God's army. Yet I have special gifts and strengths which enable me to walk this path which is often lonely and full of mystery. I hope to help as many as possible during this short visit in this mortal coil.

That is my focus.

Pray for Hilary's son.
Pray for whoever killed her.
Pray for my partner
Pray for my Mum
Pray for my children
Pray for my friends

Pray for Lin
Pray for her family
Pray for my perceived enemies and look for the lessons in
*   forgiving them.*
Love to you Lin.

20th March 2015
*   Brave, brave Lin.*
*   Tiger warrior.*
*   Elemental force guiding you*
*   Through the forests of the night.*

*   What immortal hand or eye*
*   Dare frame thy symmetry.*
*   What kind of symmetry Lin?*

*   Fearful.*
*   Brave on.*
*   Brave through.*
*   Brave be.*

*   Your sister in Love and Courage*

Hotel Seehof in Charlottenburg, Berlin
17th May 2015

(Clara was sitting alone in the restaurant of Hotel Seehof in Charlottenburg, Berlin. We recognised each other instantly, despite having met only briefly last November.

We hugged. I gave her a pink silk scarf, full of flowers. On my return from the bathroom, she told me the following.)

[The scarf] is powerful because it's confirmation that I'm a precious human and that my voice should be kept well and that I do have a voice and that it's worth something. As soon as I feel the silk around my neck, I realised that it's what I should be wearing around my neck. I knew that you'd be bringing it for me, and I knew that there was something profound about the healing.

On the way here, I was thinking to myself how I should tell my story. I don't want to talk about my drama, really. I want my contribution to be of help to any survivor. Not going over the gory details – I've had some grave experiences in my life – but what's more important is how I've come through this.

One of the tools for me is having a conversation with my "higher cause" or what I call *Strömung* in German, or flow. If I had been taught as a child to pray, to meditate, there would been somewhere for me, in my head, to go.

I've been working all of my life, banging on doors metaphorically. Looking for help, looking for sympathy, looking for confirmation, in a way. Yes, I've been such a victim, but I'm not anymore.

A very good friend of my father passed away recently. He once invited me to go to Paris, made me a guest in his city, and tried to get into my pants too. He told me I was a victim, and that I was too old to change. He told me he would have liked to help me, but he would not because I was a victim.

I choke a lot recently. It's all connected with speaking. I'm talking about speaking authentically. It's amazing: when I have another asthmatic attack, I know now what to do. I get on my knees and pray.

The scarf is wrapping my voice, something beautiful and fine, something valuable. That's significant.

I'm coming to the process of healing. I noticed that as May started, and I knew that you were coming, I was dramatising things, trivial things. The gory details of my life is a book in itself, or two.

My mom told me after I came back from living and working on the streets – they had picked me out, I'm lucky I got away – my mom told me that I had had a "temporary lapse of reason".

I was 18. I had been away for about a year. In Canada.

One recurring thread throughout my adolescent and adulthood was the threat of terror. Unhealed trauma. Terror that they'll come and get me. Terror that they'll know it's me.

One of the biggest things is I'd say to myself, "Don't be silly; you're getting carried away."

MY PARENTS

I know that my father never intended me any harm but he was a specialist for the occult.

My mother is a gentle, simple, intelligent person. She was abducted as a child on the way home from school with her sister, and then she was returned. Same day service. She has never processed it. I don't know the extent of her suffering but she was definitely abused by the man who took her. The man had told her, "Your mom told me to get you from school."

Her sister ran away when the man approached them. She saw a bobby[1] and she said to him, "That man's taking my sister away."

My mom told me that the man had told her: "Yeah, I bet you soiled your knickers. Show me your knickers."

She must have been either eight or nine. But she had always played it down. She'd say, "But they got me before the man did anything bad to me." As far as I am concerned, Lin, the damage was done regardless of what did, or did not, happen.

My sister was also abused. We had a babysitter.

We emigrated to Canada when I was three and a half years old. When I was eight, my parents divorced, which was rare back then.

I don't know whether my dad did anything to me. He had strange people, students, around. My mom had had enough of his antics; he had an affair with an 18-year-old *au pair* girl who was working for friends, and my mum threw him out. Then we were alone. That happened on the day of my eighth birthday.

---

1 A bobby is British slang for a police officer.

In my house, a lot of things happened. We had an Ouija board, all sorts of paraphernalia. It was a scary basement.

My dad taught me from a very early age to protect myself, how to put a spell on someone. That was a lot of information for a little kid on what to do: when somebody's infringing on my boundaries, he taught me how to give them an evil eye.

My dad, in those circles, was a highly-regarded magus. I couldn't have a normal childhood, growing up in a conservative province in Canada. I don't remember anything specifically evil. But I saw a lot of stuff, in terms of voodoo and working with figurines.

My dad was a professor. He was a loving person and had many students who really adored him. He was a mentor to many. He was a prisoner of war during the Korean war. The Chinese captors put a tattoo on his arm. He was with the French Foreign Legion at the age of 17. He was shanghaied against his will when he was with the merchant navy on a stop in Marseille.

As a child, he was a victim of severe physical abuse. His aunt told me, at his funeral, that he ran away at the age of four because his mother used to beat him up heavily. His aunt used to protect him and he lived with his grandmother for a while. My dad's grandmother was a herbal doctor. She knew enough that if a woman got pregnant during the war, she could concoct something that would result in an abortion. She was what my father would call a witch.

My dad was a genius. He had a photographic memory. He wrote an entire play on Shakespeare in Shakespearean verse. He was a very bright man, a beautiful soul, but all messed up. He couldn't process all that had happened to him.

He was in the merchant navy at the age of 14. He had plenty of trauma because that was our family. Plenty of talented, traumatised souls.

My mother was raised a Baptist, although she did not practise. She is an atheist today. She is also a beautiful, gentle soul whom people love dearly.

I really wish that I could have had a strong connection with her. My victim status still gets in the way of that, Lin. Despite being in recovery all this time.

MY ABUSE

We had a babysitter from next door. His window was adjacent to mine, three metres away, which was a source of dread to me. He was 14, I was eight or nine and my sister was three years younger than me. She recalled graphically that he had intercourse with her. She must have been five or so. I don't remember that – I did not witness it and if I did, I don't know it now.

My sister tried to report him about 10 years ago. The police had called me once. This was eight years ago. I couldn't be a proper witness because I couldn't give a proper testimony. My memory does not serve me well regarding her abuse.

I remember my sister coming to my bed all the time because of the monster under the bed. We were terrified kids. Totally neurotic.

Which was why alcohol was perfect. I was addicted to codeine at the age of eight or nine. Anything that would numb me. From the age of nine, we had lodgers who lived in the basement so my mom could pay the mortgage.

I remember one night, I had a girlfriend over and I could hear her whimpering. One man had come upstairs. I woke up and felt a naked man sleeping next to me. A stranger. An adult. I was a little girl.

At that moment, I had my first conscious out-of-the-body experience. I created an illusion that there was a place in that wall that I could crawl into, to get away. I went in there, amidst the cans of food.

Hotel Seehof in Charlottenburg, Berlin
18th May 2015

FAMILY SECRETS

I don't think I have ever told my mom. I do remember he had black, curly hair and a hairy body. I don't remember it being dealt with. The thing with my family is that we don't talk about these "family secrets".

I have still not confronted her after twelve years in recovery from alcoholism. My mom once told me to my face, when I got sober 12 years ago, at a big family party, "It's not true. You're not an alcoholic. You're looking for a way to escape from your problems."

It was when I got sober that everything fell apart. Shortly before I got sober, I knew that I couldn't continue running away from myself. I had paranoia, my behaviour was psychotic and I had delusions I was being followed everywhere. I was always convinced that the KGB[2] was following me, that someone was always following me. I didn't know then that I was losing my sense of reality, but I knew I was in hell.

---

2   The KGB is an acronym for the foreign intelligence and domestic security agency of the USSR.

Looking back, it all happened as it should have in order for me to surrender my old way of dealing with my trauma. But I wasn't aware that that was happening to me.

A CHILD PROSTITUTE

I was always terrified of being found out, that my kids would find out that I was forced to work on the streets as a teen.

My mom said, "Don't ever tell anyone," after I came home from living on the streets as a forced sex slave.

My dad, too, said, "Don't ever tell anyone or any man you're seeing as he would not be able to deal it. You must never let anyone know what you have done."

They were so ashamed. More secrets.

[It began when] I started jazz dancing. I was 14. I was pretty underdeveloped as my breasts were small. I was at this alternative academic school where everyone's parents were rich. My girlfriend, Stacy, and I, we were the only ones whose parents were divorced. I knew I was being mobbed. That sense of being a victim was always there with me like a bad smell you cannot get rid of because you don't know where it comes from.

I was a school actress; I did all the female lead acting roles. I had a grade nine teacher. At the end of school, he called me to the front of the class. I thought that perhaps I had done well again, that's why he had called me first.

He put his finger next to my mark. He'd given me 38 percent! I started crying. He started laughing. He said, "You see, so you get what you deserve."

There was another girl, Katy. Her mother had committed

suicide. After class, my teacher took all three of us – Katy, Stacy and I – and told us, "You'll never make anything out of your lives because you come from broken homes."

Katy kicked him. But I sided with my teacher, that Stockholm syndrome. You know because of my dad and what happened at home. I had read about Stockholm syndrome, about siding with the captors. I've suffered from this since I was very, very young. I was struggling. How was I supposed to go to high school now?

I had to do remedial lessons. My teacher changed my mark. Anyway, I ended up going to this school that I didn't want to go to because it was too big; it was real life. I had no means of going to an alternative academic school, which is what I wanted, so I ended up going to this big school and getting lost. I started dance lessons with a dance school close to the high school I was attending.

The dance teacher took us to Las Vegas. There were three students whose parents allowed them to go along with her: Kandy, Debbie and I. At the age of 15, to see a dancer's lifestyle, over a long weekend of four to five days, it was something.

We stayed with two choreographers who were also cocaine addicts. Yes, I did cocaine for the first time. It was amazing to be awake all night, lose weight and feel powerful and confident too.

At the dance school, everyone was on diet pills and watching their weight. I was taking diet pills, but they made me edgy. That's when alcohol was great because it calmed me down.

I went to dance class three times a week. My dance teacher

had another young "lady", a couple of years older than me – Mary Jay. She had a lot of friends, black men from the States. Mary Jay took us clubbing maybe when I was 16. Was it OK? No, but we got in somehow. I felt important, like how a grown-up might feel.

Mary Jay's friends called themselves "stateside niggers". A lot of them had been football players in the States. They were boxers, sports champions, students: "mean motherfuckers". There was a whole lot of new language I got trained in. They were pimps. People who, when caught by the police, would be charged with "living off the avails of prostitution". Real criminals whom I sympathised with because I suffered from the Stockholm syndrome, typical of victims of abuse.

One of them, Richie, I thought, was very good because he had big brown sad eyes. How naïve I was. He had a well-oiled afro. He gave me a teddy bear and a gold necklace. He took me out to dinner.

I remember him telling me, "Clara, I've done something for you now. You need to do something for me now. I bought you food, a teddy bear and a gold necklace. You've got to do something for me. You need to get live for me."

I remember his voice changing, he started sucking his teeth when he spoke. He said, "Yeah, because it's 'The Game'. Because now, you owe me. Because we're gonna turn you out. We know where your family lives. And we will have to visit them if you don't do what we say."

Mary Jay was a key figure in the whole thing. She said, "You've got to do what he says." Mary Jay made it clear that you don't mess with this guy – he's one of what they called "live niggers". She said, "You don't have to go alone to turn your first trick."

So she sent me and a girl named Lizzy. She was terrified too. She was what they called a "mark" because her parents were really rich. They thought they could get a lot of money from her. So I went with Lizzy to a fancy, high-class restaurant. It was dark.

The owner of the restaurant was there as he had been informed that we were coming. We were told to go with him upstairs. I had to go down on him to perform fellatio and I was given a hundred dollars afterwards. Maybe Mary Jay was there, I don't remember. I had to take the money and pass it on. We would get some pocket money. I guess Richie got it.

He told me, "OK, now you've done it, now there's no turning back. Once a 'hoe' (whore), always a hoe... and I'll protect you. You are one of my bitches!"

I realised then that I was caught and I was terrified. I didn't go to the police and I didn't go to my mom. Those men were very violent people. They carried guns and knives and had tough women in their "stables" who lived on the streets and who were used to drugs, violence and crime.

It was October. I had just turned 17.

"We know where your family lives." I could not protect my mum from being alone as a single mum, I could not protect my sister from the babysitter who raped her, and now criminals willing to sell young girls for money were threatening my beloved family.

The only way I could cope was getting drunk. It was so terrifying – it was the world at large, at last. It was much too big and dangerous for me.

an email
13th January 2016

Dear Lin,

I would like to add some important words after reading through this.

It is now a year since our meeting in Berlin. So much has happened, and is happening as I write this.

I am still struggling to let go of these old ideas that keep me emotionally crippled. I have recently hit another low, have encountered myself and recognise the selfish nature of my ego. It wants me to remain a victim. Change is so frightening. I fear not changing though. I know that I must change or die. I know that a lot of women and men who suffered abuse and also alcoholism or drug addiction do not make it.

Getting away from alcohol was incredibly difficult, as was giving up cigarettes. This new challenge, to lay down the toolkit that being a victim has offered me, is much more demanding. I recently gave up sugar, and yesterday I just needed a piece of chocolate. I allowed myself that, even though I know it is not helpful for my emotional growth.

I must be gentle with myself. I am very, very hard on myself, like my abusers were. I realise that in being a victim, I am also an abuser: in relationships, where I feel like a victim – I make the other the abuser, and am therefore abusing. It is complex.

One thing I know for sure is that I want to live, not die. I want to share my experience, strength and hope with others. I want to blossom and become the woman God created me to be.

I know that it is possible. I will not give up. I do know that it is a long, rocky road though for those of us who have suffered abuse.

Louise Hay[3] is an amazing example of someone who has healed and continues to heal, helping others along the way. She started her publishing company when she was over 50. She never completed high school. I was listening to her affirmations today. She gives me hope that I may pass on to others who find hope in my voice.

I have just finished recording an album; we are anticipating success with it. I have a beautiful home. I have loving friends. My three children are splendid humans, with an open perspective to a healed life. I am friends with my ex-husband. My mum turned 80 yesterday, and I feel so much love and compassion for her, for that little girl who was taken by a stranger as a child.

My customers in the shop love me. I am the heart and soul of all that I do. I bring a lot of good things to the table. I am healing, Lin. You have been a huge part of this process. Thank you for holding my hand as I let go of the security of smallness and receive the wondrous miracle of greatness.

I pray that anyone who reads this book finds identification, courage, hope – that they may choose, upon reading this to say out loud: "I am a beautiful, unashamed child of God and now receive the healing, goodness and prosperity that is mine."

---

3 Hay was an American motivational author and speaker. She passed away on 30th August 2017.

A NOTE FROM CLARA

If I could say something directly to the reader as an afterword:

If you suffered as a child, you are not alone. I am an alcoholic who has not drunk in over 12 years, who is healing the wounds of my turbulent and traumatic childhood without having to numb the pain with alcohol, pills, or drugs of any kind. You, too, can heal your life and become happy, joyous and free like I did.

There is a way, and it starts with becoming aware of the pain. No matter what, keep asking for help. If you are too ashamed to ask out loud, ask in your prayers at night and in the morning, and all through the day. Your prayers will always be heard. Mine were.

You will meet the teachers you need to recover as you are ready to heal, and not before. There is nothing bad or good that will last for too long; every pain passes and the pain is a blessing if taken straight without additives.

If I can do it, you can do it. All you have to do is ask. God bless you and keep you always.

Healing and working through this material is a process that takes years and years. Many are in too much pain to look into this mirror. Many take their own lives, or get caught up with alcohol, drugs, cancer, Alzheimer's and other illnesses in order not to look at what has plagued this planet.

In my opinion, the damage is microcellular and the ego has had to work so hard to create an armour in the first place, that undoing the armour and putting aside the safety of the shackles that bind us in victimhood requires incredible courage – courage which is only available within the secure foundation of a united cause.

You are amazing, Lin. What a privilege it is to know you, and to be a part of this monumental contribution to humankind. Thank you for your incredible patience in waiting for my edits, and thanks be to the Divine Spirit which has granted you both the inspiration and the courage to compile such a work.

The fact that this book you are compiling benefits a non-governmental organisation such as YAKIN (Youth, Adult survivors & Kin In Need), and is not a capitalist venture, further protects the survivors while also benefiting the reader.

We are not being used for the profit of one person. We are all able in this way to contribute to a greater good, by helping with our stories. This aspect truly aids in finding forgiveness by empowering us, by giving our voices a value which can benefit all, whether they read the book, donate to YAKIN, and/or have relatives and friends who have received relief from the higher vibrations provided from healing.

The aspect of anonymity is essential. If I had had the slightest notion that my identity would not be held sacred, I would have been unable to reveal my wounds to you. The voice you have given me with this publication comes from that little girl deep, deep within who has hidden behind the cloaks of pain, the guise of victimhood – and so she who needed to be heard when she was hurt has spoken, and the words on paper become her Truth. Someone has listened. Someone has taken notes. Someone is identifying. Someone is healing. Now I have it on paper.

It is my opinion that the collected value of this work is truly Nobel Peace Prize material – with no exaggeration. The evil energy behind child abuse can be extinguished by the love of surrender and forgiveness, but awareness has to come first!

It is, strangely enough, the abusers who are the greatest victims in the end. In all likelihood, they were also abused as children, and hurt people hurt people. So may this book find them too, that they may find themselves and in so doing seek forgiveness.

We must evolve. We must love one another. We must forgive. Without forgiveness, healing is not possible.

Thank you, thank you, thank you.

MICHAEL

41-year-old Michael was born and brought up in the Midwest in the United States, and currently lives in California. He owns a company in the entertainment industry. As a child, Michael was abused over several years by multiple people: his grandmother, his father, his brother, a babysitter and several teenagers in his neighbourhood. He is single.

....

a teleconversation, Los Angeles
1st December 2015

A pretty good place to start would be the different levels of awareness. Some are clear, some are shadowy. I'll start with the clearer ones.

DRAWINGS
The things I remember have to do with my dad. With him, it's a lot of body reactions and visual flashes and nightmares – a ton of nightmares where he is trying to molest me. In the

dreams, I'm watching TV with my dad on a pull-out bed, and something on the TV becomes sexual and he gets turned on, and then he wants to touch me.

This is a dream, one that I've had many times.

When I visited my parents and looked at old photo albums, I saw photos of me as a baby on that pull-out bed with my dad, and it was disturbing for me to see. I'd feel it in my body, that uneasy feeling.

Also, when I was a kid, I had night terrors and my parents would wake up, soothe me, and try to put me back to sleep. Part of the night terrors was that there was a witch at the bottom of my bed and I thought if I'd stay still, I would be invisible somehow and not get hurt. I don't know if the witch was real or just in my imagination, but that was the thing – if I'd stay still, I won't get hurt. Maybe this was an image to represent my dad molesting me at night, but I don't know.

Something that has helped me a lot is writing with my left hand. It's a way to bypass your conscious mind – it bypasses the filter that wants to censor the inner child. I'd ask my inner child questions and he then answers through drawings and writings. The handwriting's very poor because it's my left hand.

My dad is in a lot of these drawings, doing very sexual things to me. Forced oral sex, anal rape. I was very small and he was huge.

In these drawings – left-hand drawings – he's on top and I'm face down on a couch, and I'm seeing the scene from the side or floating above, disassociated from what's happening. These aren't normal memories, but just what has come out in the left-hand drawings.

I was maybe four or five. Things at home and in the neighbourhood were happening all at the same time. I don't know if what was portrayed in the drawings actually took place or not, but if I had a friend telling me all this, I'd immediately assume that it was all real. From an outside perspective, it's easier to put all the clues together, but for me, in my head, I have so much doubt about what was real or not.

Another thing that would happen is a recurring dream about oral sex.

I would have a dream where I would curl down and give myself oral sex. What is weird is that in the dream, I know exactly how it feels to have a penis in my mouth, even though that's not something I've done in real life, as an adult. But it's a recurring dream so I wonder if the drawings about the forced oral sex are real memories, because I also have dreams about it.

Another thing, a body reaction, is that there were times when I was around my dad as an adult, I would bleed from my rectum. So I wondered if my body was remembering something my mind was afraid to remember. I'd also get chronic coughs around him, as if I'm trying to cough up and get rid of something, or maybe an old body memory of an oral rape, I don't know. There aren't clear memories but are really consistent bodily reactions when I would visit my dad.

When I was working on forgiveness, I decided to ask my dad about his past, what happened in his childhood. He told me many stories of being abused and seeing abuse in his neighbourhood. Unfortunately, he lies a lot so it's hard to tell what's true or not. But these are the stories about his childhood that he told me:

One time, he and his brother were caught in an alley with a girl. His brother was trying to rape the girl and they got caught. As a punishment, their dad – my grandfather – whipped them with a belt as they were lying face down, naked, on their beds. So the link between sex and violence is strong for my dad. That position, being face down, is something that comes up a lot in my drawings, so I wondered if that was an abuse position he later then perpetrated on me.

He also said he was sexually active in fourth grade, that he had a boyfriend and they had sex. That was hard for me to comprehend, being that young and sexually active.

He also told me a story about him watching his brother have sex with a neighbour boy in their bedroom. That memory is strange because my dad is just standing there, observing what his brother was doing. Sometimes I think maybe that it was happening to him, not the neighbour, and that he had left his body and was watching the trauma happen from the outside.

Another story was seeing another neighbour boy molest a younger boy somewhere in the neighbourhood. I don't think he knew this older boy, but later in life that same neighbour boy was convicted for pedophilia.

He also told me about being raped by a professor when was drunk in college. His professor gave him a ride home, took him inside, and raped him, and then my dad's mother, my grandmother, walked in and saw this happening. She later blamed my dad for what had happened and accused him of being gay.

Some of the stories don't add up and in all of them, he is the victim. He tends towards the psychopathic side, so it's hard to tell what's a story and what is fiction.

EMOTIONAL INCEST

The thing with my dad which is completely clear is the emotional incest. He started sharing details about his sex life, sexual fantasies and pornography when I became an adult, around 19 or 20 years old. And it escalated over the next few years.

I hit my breaking point in my late twenties.

The breaking point for me was two things. I was 28 or 27 and we were having a conversation on the phone. We were joking around when he told me that he injected his penis with a drug in order to masturbate. I laughed it off, thinking it was a crazy joke, but he said it was real. It was disturbing.

The other thing was another phone call. He called, scared. He had been looking at pornography online and then clicked on a website that had child porn. He was scared that he would be caught and get arrested for it. I was in shock hearing this, and defaulted to my care-taking mode. I told him how to clear his cache.

That was very painful in my memory, to realise that the man who raised me, and had access to me as a child, was looking at child pornography.

I know he's a sex addict, a porn addict. He can't stop bringing up sex into any conversation he can, and often it drifts to talking about boys, young boys. Often my mom threatens to leave him, and when she does, he cleans up his act for a while, and she decides to stay. That's been their pattern my whole life. They've been together 47, 48 years now.

So I think about all the factors, his attraction to boys, the thing with the website, his sex addiction, his sexual trauma, and add to that the nightmares that I have, the left-hand drawings, and the grossed-out feeling when I'm around him...

When I add all of that up, it's pretty clear that he probably abused me.

DREAMS

I had reccurring nightmares of being attacked by invisible forces, ghosts, and later malicious strangers. I'd try to fight back, but no matter how much I hit them, they were invincible; my beatings had no discernible impact.

The further I got into therapy, the more I felt I was getting closer to recognising who these people were, the identity of my attackers. In a meditation, I set an intention and asked "Can I see the face of my abuser?" I drifted asleep and saw a face very clearly. I drew a man with a moustache and a round face. I didn't know who it was, but the image was clear.

Several months later, I was flipping through a family photo album and I was shocked to find the face. It was my uncle, my mom's brother. It was a photo from the 1980s and it was the face from my dream. When I drew the face, I didn't recognise him, but the similarity was outstanding.

I asked my mom about her brother, what his childhood

was like. She said when they were in Catholic schools, he spent a lot of time with a priest who was later convicted for paedophilia, so we guessed that he had been abused by this priest. He had a lot of signs of someone who was abused: the perfectionism, rigidity, and he possessed this layer of self-righteousness vis-à-vis his siblings, many of whom struggled with addiction and alcoholism. In context, I could see that these were walls he put up to feel OK about himself because he probably felt so ashamed inside from the sex abuse he had gone through.

But it seemed like he was perpetuating the abuse too, passing it down to the next generation.

There was one time he was at a party at my other uncle's house. He was in the basement with my younger cousin who has Down's syndrome. Her mom walked down into the basement and got upset, accusing my uncle of molesting her daughter. He got defensive and said he wasn't doing anything, but it's certainly a strange thing to be accused of unless something weird was happening.

Also, the way my uncle treats his own daughter – like a princess, and more like a partner than a daughter. Blatant emotional incest, and maybe he's abusing her too.

So when I asked my mom about him, she told me these things and unfortunately admitted that he babysat me and my brother a lot when we were little kids. So he would have had ample opportunity to abuse us.

SEXUAL HEALING

My next source of information is from guided meditations. I was listening to a recording on "Sexual Healing" by Peter Levine, a pioneer in trauma healing from Colorado.

In the meditation, the goal is to focus on my body and see what sensations come up. In this meditation, I started to feel a tingling in my groin, which spread out to my thighs, the back of my thighs and it started to feel wet. I started to have a body memory maybe of getting my diaper changed as a baby. In that memory, I saw a flashback of an older woman who was sick, my mom's mom, whom I barely remember because she died young. In this flashback, she was changing my diaper and then shoving her finger into my anus.

I don't know if that was actually happened or not, but those were the images and sensations that came up. What I do know is that my grandma was very sick – she was mentally ill – and became addicted to drugs. She herself had been sexually abused by her dad and brother, my great-grandpa and granduncle. She was a victim, who then abused one of her sons, my uncle – a different one from the one who was abused by the priest.

So I can see how the abuse is generational, and also perpetrated throughout the community.

DREAM WORK

I've had some other flashbacks come up in my trauma work and I don't know where they fit.

In one, I saw a naked boy standing, scared, and somebody reaching for his penis. It was a vague image. I don't know whether it was happening to me, or something I had witnessed. There was no context, just that image.

Another flash – a visual flash – happened one night when I was writing in my journal. Some intense feelings came up and I was doing left-hand writing in my journal and I started to hallucinate blood on the page of the journal.

Blood and shit.

Then I had a mental flash of seeing myself taking my own underwear off, as a child, and seeing blood and shit in my underwear, like I had been raped. Again, I don't know the context: my age, where I was, what happened, but just that image coming through and it was very clear.

At that time, in general, I was doing a lot of trauma work – therapy, somatic experiencing, cranial-sacral, and other body work. Part of this work was choosing a "resource": a strong place or image or set of images to focus on when I was feeling overwhelmed by the feelings from the trauma. The images I chose were the X-Men.

I read comics when I was a kid, so the images of these superheroes were very empowering, very comforting to me. So when I was feeling dizzy or disoriented or disassociated from my trauma work, I'd focus on the X-Men and started to feel centred again.

There was a period of time in LA I was doing this trauma work and using the X-Men as a resource when it really empowered me, like physically empowered me. I was focusing on the feelings of rage at my abusers, not even being clear who they were, but just feeling rage at how they had hurt me.

I was living next to a running trail and I'd run and focus on the X-Men, particularly Phoenix. I would picture Phoenix – that bird of fire burning out of my chest – and I could run really fast. Faster than I've ever run before. I felt unlimited energy and sprinted faster and longer than I ever had. I knew I was releasing that rage, that energy that I'd pent up all these years, releasing it through this powerful image and through a safe activity like sprinting.

Turning that frozen trauma energy into fight and flight, and discharging it was very cathartic.

That resource work started to come into my nightmares too, empowering me. I was able to turn into the Phoenix in my dreams and fight the perpetrators. They could shoot me, attack me, try to molest me and I could burst into this powerful fire and charge right at them.

I was taking my power back: in my dreams and in real life.

MY DAD

Also as part of my therapy work, I decided to take a break from seeing my dad. I didn't know how long I would do this, but it ended up being three years. I had a friend who had a similar dad – a sex addict father who was also using drugs and had bad boundaries. When she stopped talking to him, she felt much better. It was inspiring, so I tried it.

Before I stopped talking to him, I was getting more and more angry at him. Real deep rage. One night I was talking to him about a creative project and he shot it down in a passive-aggressive way. The subject didn't matter so much, it was just me getting so fed up with his mind games. I got so mad at him. I went to bed and was thinking "I want to kill him", to literally murder him.

I had to think it through and realise no matter how right

it felt in the moment to want to kill him, I knew it wouldn't be the right thing. I slept on it and felt better in the morning, but that amount of rage was scary. I knew I needed to take a break from seeing him, otherwise I was going to end up either hurting him or myself.

My final visit to him, before the three-year break, was around 2011. I had just got in from the airport and I was standing in the kitchen. I looked over at him and saw him looking at my crotch.

I tried to deny it in my mind, but I couldn't anymore. I had to accept he was a sexual predator and most likely had abused me when I was a child. I felt horrible that night, like the earth opened up and I fell in. I knew I couldn't keep visiting him. So that was my last visit for the next three years.

During that time, I did a ton of therapy and trauma work. Not seeing him gave me the space to feel my rage and not be afraid that I was going to hurt him. I didn't have to pretend or be social with him while feeling this rage and hurt and grief. Even from afar, he kept playing his games. He slowly turned my brother against me. He also raped my mother a few times in her sleep.

He does these things and is able to spin it like he is the victim. I'm pretty sure now he is a sociopath, that he doesn't feel empathy, or much at all.

ACCEPTANCE

After three years, I decided to reconnect with him. In some ways, it got to the point where being in partial contact was easier than holding up the wall of having no contact. I had given myself a lot of time to feel things and heal, and I naturally was moving towards acceptance.

I can accept he is a sex addict, a predator, a sociopath, and that he'll never change. I'm an adult now and can protect myself from him. Also, as he's getting older, he has less energy to play his mind games. For a long time, I was so scared of seeing him again and kept trying to figure out what the perfect armour would be to protect myself against him.

My revelation was that there is no perfect armour, against him, or anything bad in the world. I'm going to feel pain, but I can survive pain, and pain makes me more fearless. So I do see him again, and I have very low expectations when I do. And when he says something inappropriate, it hurts, but it doesn't kill me, and I have a lot of friends around me who support and love me that I can rely on. I don't need to rely on my dad anymore for that need for family.

A NOTE FROM MICHAEL

The best way to sum up the work I've done to heal is say: "I've tried everything."

I've thrown everything I can find at the problem and to be honest, I don't know what specific methods worked, just that I've gotten better. I've found that when anyone tries everything at their disposal, things get better. The key ingredient, which can be the most elusive, is willingness.

When I was in my late twenties, I knew I had issues with sex and intimacy. Even though I hadn't had many nightmares or flashbacks yet, I knew something was wrong.

I was chronically picking unavailable women who were often sex addicts, and often cheated on me. I was subconsciously choosing partners who would re-create that feeling of sexual betrayal I felt over and over in my childhood, because I was being abused by someone whom I was supposed to trust.

But even with that pain, I wasn't yet willing to pick up the tools I needed to start healing. That willingness came during Easter of 2005.

I was visiting my family in the Midwest and there was a report on the news about a girl who had been kidnapped. As the news came out, it was a young girl who had lived in the same neighbourhood I had grown up in. A day or two passed, and she was found raped and murdered by a paedophile, who also lived in that neighbourhood and was friends with her mother.

When that happened – this took place in my old neighbourhood, on the very streets that I grew up on – something in me changed.

I started to realise this didn't happen in isolation and the few snippets I could remember or the discomfort I felt about sex and intimacy were no long just this random thing. I started to see cause and effect: that the pain I felt, that feeling of being permanently broken inside, maybe came from the fact that I came from this place, this neighbourhood, this culture of it being OK for children to be sexualised and touched and molested and raped. And my deepest fear was that maybe I was a victim, and if so, that maybe I'd become a perpetrator too. I knew enough about the cycles of violence to know that – victims could become the next generation of perpetrators if they don't heal.

I felt like I had few options, and none of them were attractive.

The first was to deny that there was a problem and keep hoping things would just fix themselves. But I kept having more and more mental flashbacks of the abuse. The problem was finding me.

And what do I do with these flashbacks? They were awful – flashbacks and images of children being sexualised, or molested. I felt like a monster just having these images in my head, because at the time I didn't realise they were memories. I thought it was something I wanted, that maybe I was a paedophile. So the idea that it would just go away on its own was something that clearly wasn't going to work, because I couldn't stop the inevitable fact that my mind was going to be releasing these images from my past. The only thing I could do is decide how I would respond to them.

The next option, to deal with these images, would be to try to just shut down my entire sex life and sex drive. I saw my dad do this, over and over, as I was growing up. At different times he took estrogen and tranquilisers to try to squash his libido, to become asexual, or a term I learnt later in life: sexually anorexic. You can see the logic: sex is bad, so get rid of your lust. And I've certainly fallen into cycles of this, being sexually anorexic. Thinking that if I do anything sexual, someone else or I was going to get hurt. Heartbroken, betrayed, disappointed, whatever, but giving up on sex and intimacy because it had become too painful.

On the flipside of that was to give in to the impulses. I've seen my father do this too, to give up trying to control his lust and diving into the darkness. For him, it was pornography, and that is also something I've struggled with when I'm feeling too scared to date real women, but wanting to feel something sexual. But these are the times I saw my dad become the most dangerous to himself and others. This was when he called me confessing about the child porn. He had given in to the images and lust in his head, given in to this idea that he was a monster, and got as dark as he could with his sexuality and lust.

So on one side was restriction, control, anorexia, and the other side was giving in, becoming dark, and diving deep into pornography or acting out sexually. And the reality of it was over the years, I was actually vacillating between these two worlds – being good, being bad, being good, being bad. These two things would support each other. I'd act out, feel bad, then go to acting in, being good. Then I'd get sick of trying to control my lust, or get worn down, give up, and go on a binge. That was the insanity of all that abuse coming to the forefront and not knowing what to do.

And finally the third option, which was healing. The slow trudge through the memories, the therapy, the spiritual work, the resourcing, the group therapy, reading book after book, doing writing exercises, having painfully awkward and honest conversations with family members and friends, and sticking with it, month after month, year and year, even when things seemed to get worse, not better, because the other options were to be anorexic or be consumed with lust. That is where my willingness came in.

These are the things that helped me, but really, each person has their own path. Some things that worked for me didn't work for my friends and vice versa. It doesn't really matter what the methods are, what matters is that I kept trying and searching and finding things that might work, and I slowly got better.

A huge part of my healing is somatic experiencing, a trauma method by Peter Levine. I've also done some eye movement desensitisation and reprocessing (EMDR) trauma healing, and have had friends get great results from it as well. I did cranial-sacral bodywork, a sort of light massage on my head that balances out the flow of spinal fluid. I'd always feel very clear and centred after those sessions, a huge contrast to the dizziness and disorientation I often felt.

I did left-hand drawing and writing when I was feeling "weird" or not myself, and it was usually an old thing from the past coming up to express itself. I did inner child work, talking to that little kid who was abused and saying to him the things he needed to hear back then – becoming my own parent essentially, re-parenting myself with the tools my parents didn't have. I got involved with spiritual paths that I liked, and for me that was Taoism, some Buddhism, meditating, some Christian prayer work. I got massages, Reiki, energy healing, tapping, pretty much anything that came my way that I thought was reasonable.

And particularly with the body work, I don't necessarily think any one method is better than others. I think the real benefit of all of it was being touched, by a safe person, week after week, in a non-sexual way. It showed me that all touch isn't sexual, something I think men, in particular, struggle with. When men are touched, it is often sexualised by everyone involved, as a joke, or as an advance. I see women hug and be comfortable with one another, and instead of feeling neglected, I chose to get regular body work so my body could get comfortable with touch too.

What I can honestly say today is that the images are gone. They came up and out and revealed themselves as what they were – echoes of abuse that happened decades ago. They weren't desires, they weren't my future, they weren't me. They were a part of a generational illness that gets passed down, parent to child, sibling to sibling, neighbour to neighbour.

Part of the gift of me doing this work to heal is that I don't just heal myself, but I heal all the generations in my lineage before me. This is profound work I got to do, and it's made me stronger than I could have ever imagined.

6

IMRAN

A diplomat from South Africa, Imran is in his early forties. He grew up in Johannesburg and was abused by a male family friend who was later murdered. He has three children and is currently working in Berlin. He is married to Nissah (see Chapter 7). All the poems in this chapter were written by him.

....

a WhatsApp conversation
12th November 2015

Imran, thanking me, for speaking to his wife: "When I got home last night, I asked how it went and she simply said, 'Don't I look lighter? This is the start of my healing.' I cried inside, thank you."

Radisson Hotel restaurant, Berlin
14th November 2015

I do not know what age I was. To be honest with you, there's still a part of me that doubts that this could be considered abuse because of who I am: a man with a family. The abuser was a close friend, as opposed to a stranger. Also, the age gap between us: he was like, two years older than me. He was bigger than me.

THE ABUSE

Feed me
8th November 2014

> *Feed me from the sap of freedom*
> *Feed me from the juice of justice*
> *Nourish my soul from the nutrients of love*
> *Enrich my being from the elements of natural being*
>
> *I wish to live as if I were at total peace that were raped*
>   *from me*
> *I wish to fly as if the soaring winds of wish were safe*
>   *beneath my fearless heart*
> *I wish to climb to the tops of peaks; of sights beyond vision*
>   *that only He may be praised*
> *Feed me for all I do is hunger*
> *Hunger until death's peaceful slumber*

It was never forced. It was never something against my will but I was confused. He exposed us to pornography.

The pornography stimulated us: "Imagine if we could do this, imagine if we could engage in this sort of activity," he would say and then you know: the detachment, the excitement, the aggression between the man and the woman. He always invited me to sleep over. Nobody thought it strange. I thought it normal. There never was penetration.

It happened over so many years and I forget how old I was... maybe between the ages of 11 and 13 when it happened.

After our first discussion, you and I, I started seeing a therapist. What I discovered was that I had a father who mentally checked out on me, who had mentally abandoned me. So there was always a desire to seek a strong male's approval. It's not something I ever got from my own father. When my abuser showed me attention and affection, and this sense of belonging – this is where I was – I was in a safe place.

THE AFTERMATH

His parents are very close to my mother. That's why I never wanted it to come out. It would have hurt that relationship. My story is not as intense as a lot of other stories but the impact of it... I have 10,000 questions: questions about my sexuality, my manliness, my alpha, my bravado. Am I man enough? I mean, it's easy to say something and it's another thing to believe, but it's too difficult sometimes. That's what made me so angry about what happened.

I'm married now. I have great kids. I have a life. My time to act now is gone because I'm comfortable with my life and I'm happy. I choose to be complacent and I'm ok with it.

I cannot go into details because I cannot remember. Although at the time, it felt good. I was stimulated and subsequent to that, my views of sex became callous, my understanding of a relationship became academic.

It is. It must be.

MARRIAGE

I have a connection with [my wife] Nissah; I love her but I just do not think I'm capable of getting and receiving love. Does she feel that? Subconsciously, I think she does. I can disappear sometimes into my own fantasy. I'll be in my own little world. I do not believe that marriage is forever. If it's great, *alhamdulillah*.[1] If it doesn't work, *alhamdulillah*.

So for me, it's not so much about what happened but the effects it has had on my life. I've always doubted myself. I'm always seeking approval and acknowledgement. I do not ever trust anybody because I cannot trust anybody and I'm aware of it. And so I become academic about it. So I start doing things: this is what a man should be, this is what a husband should be.

The thing about marriage is, there's a false conception about a partnership. Nissah's a great partner. She has her flaws, I have my flaws too. So I measure it in terms of comfort and so on. The day I realised that I was going to marry her, my brother was in Singapore and I was house-sitting and I invited her over. We were friends at the time. We watched my favourite movie and we listened to my favourite artist. And I read my poetry to her. And we sat for about an hour, not talking – there wasn't a need to talk. There was a comfortable silence. It was comfortable.

---

1 *Alhamdulillah* is Arabic for "thanks be to God".

And that's when my soul told the world that her soul would be my long-term partner. At that time, I did not know about her past; she might have known about mine. But this was exactly the place I belonged. It would be about ten years later that we would get married, but we never dated. And not for religious reasons; I don't believe in monogamous relationships. I've never believed in being faithful to a partner until my wife. I never saw any sense in it. I never saw any logic in it.

It has been a difficult journey. I'm seeing a therapist. The issue that I've been facing in therapy is the issue of guilt. And if you ask me, it's subconscious issues that people can prey on. Like they know you're vulnerable and they hone in on it. It's been an issue in our marriage. Because of her own insecurities, she can be suspicious if I meet somebody. She is insecure. If I tell her that I'm meeting somebody, she'd start feeling suspicious. And I'd feel immensely guilty and it makes me wonder whether I'm seeing someone for the right reasons. It may not even be a person, it could be social events. Even social activities.

I think you remarked once that it is a very unique thing to have two survivors married to each other. Perhaps you're right, but I also think that this works for us, because as frustrated as I am that she is so paranoid and suspicious of me, I understand her because I am like that. I do not ever trust anybody because I cannot trust anybody and I'm aware of it.

I don't trust anyone, especially myself. This is one of the consequences of abuse though, isn't it? You don't trust your actions no matter how sincere or real or altruistic they are.

You lose the ability to trust yourself, because that has been raped from you.

Because of this, all my own actions become doubt. So I question whether I've done everything to fight apartheid. And I'm guilty of the legacy of the separation of races. I'm extremely unforgiving of myself.

"What is it about my actions that made you feel insecure about me?"– that's what it is about. We do work but we are both insecure. When she doubts me, I doubt myself. We talk about it now. We work things through. I'm very proud of her. It's taken her a while to open up like this.

I've always been like this. It's like a joke in the family. When people came over to visit when I was a child, and they asked me, "Where are your parents?" I'd say, "They are in the room, working on their budget." Not realising how improper it is to say such things. Because I'm like that. Nissah is not. She's guarded. And I'm not.

We've become pedantic about things, about experiences, about appearances, about how we come across to people. Her own physical appearance is very important to her. She's concerned about her own appearance, what people think about us as a family. For me, I think it's wrong so I fight with her at every possible junction. I'm not judging her, just observations I make. I'm extremely judgemental but not judging her. I see facets in her that I see in myself. I'm protective about her. I want the best for her. I do not want her to feel bad about herself.

I want her to be happy.

HOW YOU EMBRACE IT

Scatter me
26th August 2015

Oh scatter my being, my Lord!
Scatter me amongst the vile lecherous touch of an unwanted
  man
As he rubs his erectile phallus upon my tender innocence

Oh scatter my soul, dear Lord!
Scatter me to the heated lust of a lover's scorn
As he fills his lust upon my deviance, as he enjoins the
  sanctity of my manhood with the loins of those younger
  than even me

Oh scatter my heart, dear beloved Lord!
Scatter me through the brushes of a family friend whose
  deception marries that ole clichè
As he caresses my soul for his own sick disgusting pleasure as
  I struggle now a man of age confused with my rage

Oh scatter my mind, my only Lord!
Scatter me through the rationale of right and wrong a fiend
  raped from beyond my ten year old ilm
As he licks his lips to fill my very desires of experiment versus
  abuse versus confused malaise for I know not...Is it me
  to blame?

Did I, ya Rabb,[2] call for his touch? but no kiss his release

---

2 *Rabb* is Arabic for "Lord".

of false impregnation upon my tongue to ask is this my
sexual preference or forced submission to a false god's
temptation?
Shall I for e'er more not know why I am not the same but
differ from your mainstream perception and expectation?

Suffer me more or suffer me less my grief enshrouded
through her own yet more pain and corrupted perverse
tales of horrors yet ne'er known
Why? Did he upon my soul rape from it the inner core of
the self's dared war?

Do you know me now? Do you feel empowered enough to
hurt me or betray me? Or more steal from me what little
trust in mine own true ambitions?

I should be more! I should soar higher but now I rationale
all the pain and confusion and act upon the script of
how I am supposed to feel, how I am supposed to forgive,
how I am supposed to forget but deprive myself of how
I do still feel, how I DO forgive or not or hurt or weep
or stand-alone inside my fucked up head because I don't
trust me so how to trust you or you or you or even you?

You ask far too much for my grief and healing of your life
still early stolen mine own was never more than my sweet
surrender to a darkened place I can never remember!

Am I scattered enough to answer a simple question:
Am I?

It's hard for me to talk about myself. It's hard for me to talk about what happened to me. It's like I don't know who I am, why I am and where I belong. Growing up with apartheid did not help either. Growing up in a community that was sort of like "between black and white" didn't help either. It was like: am I black or am I not black? Do I belong; do I not belong?

An obvious question that deserves an answer: Do I deserve happiness because of what happened to me? You feel the happiness and the blessings and you accept it but it becomes academic.

How you embrace it is the key. If somebody gives me a compliment, I do not know what to do with it.

COMING BACK INTO THE WORLD

The Global Diplomacy Lab (GDL)[3] was an eye-opener for me. Before I participated in the GDL, I attended the closing of the International Diplomats Programme (IDP) organised by the German Federal Foreign Office. And I made some statements there. See, that programme was me slowly coming back into the world. I had checked out mentally until then. All my successes until then was not a subconscious thing. I had some God-given talents. I could read a book and I could understand it better than others. Studying is so easy for me, especially something that I love, that I'm interested in.

I love my work – international relations I discovered late in life – I was passionate about. In the build-up to my

---

3 The GDL is a platform meant to turn diplomacy on its head, and make it more inclusive by involving non-traditional actors. The patron of the GDL is the German Foreign Minister Dr. Sigmar Gabriel. More details can be found at www.global-diplomacy-lab.org/

President's visit to Germany, I worked on my President's speeches. I wrote four of them in two hours, maybe a little more. But the speeches were based on books and texts that I had read on my own. I did not have to go over and do the research. I constantly read and I have a broad idea about texts and philosophical writers like Paulo Coelho and also religious texts, the Quran and the Hadith. It's a very important thing in my life.

GOD

My Azanian love song
for my daughter

> *Let me sing you an Azanian love song*
> *Of splendid times recorded on canvassed walls*
> *Of worlds imagined by the pens of ancient scribes*
> *Of courts of kings and queens who ruled empires of vast*
>   *great plains and koppies filled with treasures of woven*
>   *silk and golden love*
>
> *Let me sing you an Azanian love song*
> *From the mouths of genocide and slaughterous killings*
> *From the mouths of mindless masters who rape and plunder*
> *From the bowels of fearful hunger steeped in modern day*
>   *slavery*
>
> *Let me sing you this, my Azanian love song*
> *Her face so innocent and tears so warm*

Her touch as soft as ancient pride
Her wail to soothe the deepest corner of any man's sorrow

Let me sing you this, my Azanian love song
Her name shall mean more, much more than they will ever
*   know*
Her path shall spread beyond the depths of our meagre
*   beginnings*
Her smile shall light the darkest soul of this great land

I've sung to you this, my Azanian love song
As a homage to the drop ling of our joint loins
As a painting of the love and lust from whence she came
As applause for the comfort that one day shall be ours

Sing with me this, our Azanian love song
A song to fill the melodies of more peace and reconcile
A song to mend the hearts of once sworn enemies
A song to chime away the dust of forgotten horror

Let us sing together you and me, this great Azanian love
*   song*
Our song of hope and ululation
Our song of ancestral pride and humble celebration
Our song of great times again to come
For when that time shall surely come you will know that

Surely, Allah has listened!

God guides me. It's a very un-Islamic relationship that I have with Islam. I'm a practising Muslim – I pray five times a day, and I do my shit. Whatever needs to be done. If there's anything that I love unequivocally, it would be God. It'd be the Quran, also the *as-salah,* the prayers.

There were many questions in my life when I asked about this guy, God. I asked what the fuck was this guy up to? What is he doing with me? Why is he making the experience? Why did he do this? I believe that in as much as the human race is powerful, there's a guiding force in the universe. We experience major and minor – we do not know what is major and minor – but we experience and there's something grounding me on certain things.

CHECKING OUT

I cannot say to you when I checked out of life. I cannot say to you when I checked back into it. There were two instructors in my life – one was the greatness of the power, of the omnipotent power.

I was living in London, living by myself. I was high, not on drink but under the influence of something. I was poor. I had, like, two pennies to my name. I was stealing cigarettes from the bar I worked at. I sent Nissah a simple SMS: "Allah loves me." That's all I wrote.

To come to understand that was powerful. To come to peace that I'm not as good, not as magnanimous, as wonderful that I always believed that I was. That there's always someone out there better than me. She is one.

Back to Berlin, two years ago. Nissah and I had just gone

through our worst financial period, even on a posting. So we got there financially, started stabilising ourselves. An opportunity came for this programme from the German Federal Foreign Office. And it's for a junior diplomat so there's three of us, and I started enumerating my strengths and ensuring that I was the one that should apply to the programme. And I went to the interview, read my panellists' faces and got into the International Diplomats Programme (IDP).

Again at the IDP, subconsciously, I started being myself. When I asked a question, I could not care what others thought, or the role of diplomacy, or how diplomats had to behave in a certain way. IDP was when those things were manifesting: my identity, my credibility. People around me knew a lot more than me. Come IDP, I was still questioning myself. Was I worthy of being a part of this programme? Would people approve of me?

At the IDP itself, I organised after the closing ceremony, which was on a Thursday night, for everyone to come the next day to the Embassy for a *braai*, a barbeque. I just did it. We had this Israeli diplomat and the Arab diplomats, so the only place where we could all meet is the South African Embassy. During the IDP, I heard about the other programmes, like the GDL, like the BMW Foundation's Responsible Leaders programme.

Throughout my life, before checking out, I did not try to be "the leader". I never tried to impress. I made history: I was the first black elected to the students' body. It was 1994 when we had the first democratic elections in South Africa, and I was elected in 1995 to the students' body.

Now I'm trying to say what happened to me during all of

this. I reached that point when I told you that I checked out. I did not know when it was but as I began talking to you, I realise when it was. It was when it [the abuse] stopped, that's when I checked out. When I stopped being physical. I did not understand what was going on. I felt alone, that's why I question my sexuality. It's something I've come to realise now as I'm speaking to you.

HEALING

Karma come'a callin'

> *Mamma! Mamma! Mamma!*
> *What chile? What?*
> *Mamma karma come'a callin'! Mamma!*
> *Who come chile? Who come?*

> *Karma mamma! Karma come'a callin'! She do!*
> *Nay chile! She kenna be comin' that sly wench karma!*
> *So what I do now mamma? When karma come callin'?*
> *Don't see her dat karma gyal chile!*

> *I no see karma mamma but she come a callin'!*
> *Mamma I scared now mamma!*
> *Help me hard mamma! Help now mamma!*
> *I were dumb mamma! I knowed not then what I do'ed*
> *   mamma!*

> *Why she come'a knocking mamma?!*

Whyyyyyyyy?!
Hush chile lest karma done hear that foolish sob now she
   will!

Mamma karma come'a callin' mamma!
She come now mamma mit da thunder and da fear
   mamma! She know no prejudice she don't no mamma,
Noooo mamma she don't know nutting she do!
She jyest come'a callin' mamma!
She callin' da priest and da sinner mamma!
She come'a callin' she do dis karma mamma
She call on da judge an da jury too aye she do
No colour she sees just a callin' she do!

What I do mamma? What I do when dat karma come'a
   callin'?
Hush chile! Rest now! Let her call now chile! She come
   when she do an' she do how she do!
Dere be nutting dear heart that your precious life kyen do!
   Let her call, let her call
For when she do, all do fall
From king and pauper and president too,
All will fall chile' yes e'en mamma do too
Karma must call now chile she must for all she do is call on
   you and me she do
That karma wench she jyest call an' call an' call

But mamma…
Hush chile, hush for karma come'a callin'.

We come back to the closing of the IDP ceremony. Several of us were involved in the panel for the latter. Was I invited or was I an afterthought? Should they invite someone else? They sent me questions beforehand, so you could prepare the answers. However, I did not prepare, I spoke from the heart. I'm trying to think about what the question was. When I responded, there was a minute's silence and then there was applause, to the point where some members of the audience were standing.

When the call for applications for the GDL came, I applied and got in. But when I read all the members' biographies, I became so scared. Why am I a part of this group? Am I worthy? Am I going to make a difference? Am I going to work out with this group? There was a girl who stuck out for me because she – you – had won an award for combating child sexual abuse. So I was thinking, what has God got for me? What's his plan?

After I spoke, the guest speaker at the IDP closing ceremony had said, "Watch this guy. He is going to be someone. You haven't heard the last of him." All the fears I told you about disappeared. I said to myself, "You know what, Imran, you need to stop worrying about these fears and accept who you are. You are in this group because you belong there, and you need to stop holding back. You have a unique story to tell and it's a story that none of them have heard before. And whether they accept you or not, fuck it. You are at the turning point."

I just stopped being scared. I embraced me.

Yeah, it was not easy, even subsequently. I could not do this anywhere else. It's like people do not realise when they make it. They are afraid. The moment they make it, they realise: being me, not successful, is a big thing.

But I steadily turned things around for me. I did not need to apologise for being me, for being comfortable and secure in my own skin. This is why I'm seeing a therapist – to find truth, to own myself.

If I go back to the events of two to three years ago, I was this self-defeatist person – the issues that I had with my dad, and the insecurity that he never accepted me for me; I had huge daddy issues – and conquering this incident is not the be-all and end-all of my problems. I found myself vulnerable in the situation as a child. It was easier to "give" to the abuser than to give to my dead father.

You're not the first person I'm telling my story to. I've been doing this the last two to three months because I feel good about it. I think people do not realise how good it is to talk about it. The world is concerned with physical fitness, with physical training but mental strength is lost to us because we do not use it. We have to exercise it, we have to learn to come to terms with it, to find some way.

The victim [the abuser] – he is the one who suffered the most, not me. Wherever he is now. He was murdered. I had nothing to do with it, but I felt guilty. I kind of felt like it was karma. I did not mean the bastard to suffer like that. He was carjacked. I was 25 when I moved to London and the carjacking happened shortly after I moved. He was about 27.

I cried. I wept like a baby when I heard he died. I do not know why. It's not as if I was in love with this guy. You know why? He was like someone from my family. I didn't have close cousins etc. I mean, I had cousins, but because of family politics, we were never close. That was why he was like my cousin to me.

ALL SPOKEN OUT

Tired Reflections

I did not know what I was going to say to you when I got here. But at some point, I thought maybe I should back off because Nissah's story is more powerful.

She feels unimportant because she's my wife, and not Nissah. I overprotect her and do not allow her to make mistakes because I do not want her to be hurt anymore. She's been really, really hurt. By her mother, her brother. If I had not seen it with my own eyes, I'd never imagine that a mother could do this to her own child.

Her mother's a witch, it sickens me. She has the title of grandmother to my children and Nissah fights me, against me to protect them, without her realising it. I've no regard for Nissah's family because if they took the time to know her they would be on their *mussolahs* (prayer mats in Arabic) every day, they would thank God every day and every minute of their lives for what they have in her. They fucking abuse her. And take her for granted. And all Nissah ever wanted was their approval and acceptance. They do not deserve it.

I'm done. I'm all spoken out.

Danke sehr, thank you.

Epilogue: an email
9th August 2017

I am a triumphant black man who is educated in the letters of life and streets of defiance/*South Africa in spite of her current woes manages to produce amazing tales of triumph and success.*

I am a triumphant black man whose tongue is pierced by the regales of royalty and the humility of poverty.

I am simple just me/*South Africa simply just is.*

A daddy to the three most amazing souls that God has chosen me to raise!/*A home to all who live in it.*

And in that moment of realisation my therapist read the Kipling poem, "If", to me.

So thank you for holding my hand when you didn't even realise that you were. I may not say this all the time but I am grateful to share our journey together and I am in love with how intimate our paths are. You are a select few and maybe one day you will all stand in a room together and you will recognise who you are to me and you will know why, or maybe you won't, but I know and that is all.

To paraphrase from the poem and from being South African and from a loving God:

I am a man today because my daddy was who he was and you are who you are.

For when He says: "Be", it simply is.[4]

And Allah is great indeed!

Thank you.

---

4 This is an Islamic reference to God's power of creation, from the Arabic "*kun*" (be) and "*fayakun*" (and it is).

7

NISSAH

In her thirties, Nisssah is from Witwatersrand, South Africa.
Married to another adult survivor of child sexual abuse, Imran
(see Chapter 6), she was abused by her elder brother as a child.
He later died from drowning. Nissah resides in Berlin and is
studying for a degree in business administration.

....

Hotel de Rome restaurant, Berlin
11th November 2015

THE BEGINNING

This will be the first time that I'm speaking about it since my
marriage was in trouble. It had all these underlying emotions.
Intellectually, I felt that I had dealt with it. That I was not
the victim, but obviously it affected me more than I used to
admit. I have pieces of memory – most of it was too horrible,
so I blacked them out.

We moved to our home with my mom and dad when I
was five years old. I don't know how old I was when it first
happened. I did not understand what he was doing. He

was eight years older than me. I was eight years old when it stopped, I do not know how long it continued or when it started.

It started with little things, like he'd masturbate in front of me. And he'd want me to touch him. I was scared to be alone with him, I was scared of him. I used to lock myself in the toilet or my bedroom. I would cry if my mother left. I would beg her, *anybody,* to stay. We had a live-in maid. However, there was this time when there was nobody there. She had gone back to her village. I was alone with him.

Yes, he was my brother.

When I was alone with him, I ended up locking myself up in the bathroom. I was scared. And more and more, he pushed the boundaries. And the last I remembered: he was in my bedroom and I had cried out.

It came to an end that night. I screamed. It took time for my voice to come out. My father rushed in, my mom and my other brother were there as well. I remember my father pushing and punching him against the wall.

And the worst thing was when my mother asked me, did he penetrate you? I said, no. She said, so then it's fine, we won't talk about this then. It was like, hush, hush, and all that. I do not remember anyone talking to me after that.

AFTER THE ABUSE

I was very angry with my mom for a long time. I still have my issues with that. He was my mom's favourite boy. He could do no wrong. He was the oldest.

After this incident, he shut me out and nobody spoke to

me. My mom spoke to me, but about general things. I felt bad because I had all this attention from him and after that, he did not speak to me at all.

I used to pray that he would die. I felt guilty for a long time.

HIS DEATH

I was with my mom and dad. We got a call that somebody was "ill". They did not want to say that somebody had died. We were wondering who it was, and I wished it was him.

He had drowned in a canal. He was swimming, he was a good swimmer. For me, when death comes, it is not because of this or that, but because one's time is over.

I was relieved but guilty because he had died. I had always felt the power of prayer. I had always wanted to be there for my mom because he was gone, because he was her perfect child.

When I was a teenager, I tried to approach the subject again but she switched off again. After that, I could have gone either way: I could have become a bitch or a slut easily, but I held on to my chastity until I met Imran. But I think nobody believed me, including my mom. I knew many boys but I did not let it get further than kissing.

MY JOURNEY

My journey has been difficult.

I had lost almost all of my self-confidence. Imran met me at a time when I was a lot more confident because I had my father as a supporter. He always believed in me but he died when I was doing my matriculation, or your 'A' levels. At the time I got my results, he was shot and killed.

My plan after school was, I wanted to go to a kibbutz. Imagine a Muslim girl there, you know? I did not know what to do. So I studied travel and tourism. I messed around more than anything. I was not serious about studying. I went to America, where I did a work-holiday programme. I was in Idaho at a ski resort. I travelled around a little, moving through Seattle, then New Orleans and Chicago, and ended up in New York.

We got a working visa to the UK, my friend and I. I think it was 1999 when I came back to South Africa but my intention then was to say goodbye to everyone. I wanted to get lost in Europe, but God had other plans for me.

THE LOWEST POINT

My other brother met a *maulana*[1] and it was just bad news: he basically used my brother. He was from Pakistan. It was so messed up, this period of our life. I liken him to Rasputin[2]. He tore us apart to the point where my brother eventually threw me out.

And oh, my mother, how could I have forgotten? She had gotten married to an Englishman. I had issues with the Englishman. My mother sold the house and we ended up moving in with my brother. When my brother lost it – he was learning Islam but he was so naïve – the *maulana* ended up marrying my brother's wife! She was white as well. Basically,

---

1 *Maulana* is Arabic for "religious teacher".
2 Grigori Yefimovich Rasputin was a mystic and self-proclaimed holy man who held considerable sway over the family of Tsar Nicholas II.

my brother abandoned her and this guy ended up marrying her, and my brother took his kids away. At the time, he was OK with all this.

Basically, my brother kicked my mom out, then he kicked me out. He kicked me out at night. I remember the *maulana* being there. I looked at him and I said, "Really, is this what you are doing?" I called my mom to come and get me. And I remember her saying, "What must we do? I guess we'll have to take you in now." God, I was then at my lowest point.

I was about 25 years old. I did not have a job. I ended up staying with my mom. Through all this time, I stayed in touch with Imran. I used to think that this was all my fault. This *maulana* was filling my mind about being submissive and how I should be. It went against everything I believed in. I did not want to be that. My mother was busy phoning around to get me married. To get me out, away, basically.

The person my mom was setting me up with was Imran's friend. Imran called me, asking, "Are you really marrying him?" I ended up marrying Imran instead.

That was the second proposal. The first time, he was in London and I was back home. This *maulana* was already in my life then and had taken over the role of my father. The night Imran came over, I kept quiet; I did not say a word. We ended up not getting married. The *maulana* cross-questioned him. I called it off.

The second time he asked, we decided to get married. We never really dated. I think he had always known [about my background], and I understand him, and he was always there for me. I think we bring out the worst and the best in each other. He is really a good man and I'm so glad that I met him.

He tried to bring my brother and I back together. But it happened again: my brother cut me out of his life. This is my opinion: he figured that we were not good enough Muslims. That was the real reason why he cut me out, and only if I'm in real trouble will he be there for me.

GIVING BIRTH

Imran told me that the biggest fights I've had with my mom were when I was pregnant or about to go into labour.

When I had my first child, I brought up all these underlying issues but she pushed it to the side. The day I gave birth, my mother-in-law said, "Well done, I'm so proud of you", but my mom looked at me and said, "Now you can feel how it feels."

Imran had decided on the day I gave birth to paint the rooms of the house. In our culture, for the first forty days after birth, we stay with or are helped by our mothers. My mother did not want to, first of all. But the fumes from the paint were so strong, she was forced to take me in. When I did move back home, maybe a week later, she did not come to the naming ceremony of my baby. She went on holiday with her husband instead! It was a huge thing for me; we had slaughtered an animal for a feast and to give away to the poor.

When we had our second child, my mother-in-law begged her to come. She came but because she was not the centre of attention, she threw a fit and said she was going to walk home. My mother felt neglected and decided to leave! And in fact, she did leave!

My greatest argument with her took place in Berlin. My mother came over to visit; my brother also came. And this time, my mother denied the abuse when I brought up the issue. She said, "I don't remember what you're talking about." But this brother knew about it.

When I look at my children, I think, how can I think of abusing a child? How can you look at a girl and be attracted to her?

I want to be honest with my children. They have a very different life from me. They are happy and sheltered. I do not want them to be victims. I want them to be empathetic.

I said that to my mom and my brother. We had a huge fight. I realised then they do not care about me. If my father were alive, he would not have allowed this to happen, to have them abandon me.

I accept this. She is not well-educated. She's not intelligent enough. She does love me even though she does not know how to. She lost her mom when she was twelve. Imran says that when I say these things, it's as if I am making excuses for her but I love her and I cannot deny her a relationship with my daughters. Imran is very protective. He'd say: "She doesn't deserve that. She doesn't deserve you."

I need to move on, and once and for all deal with it, and that is why I'm speaking to you today. And I know that my daughters will look at me as their role model. They are growing up quickly so I need to find my self-confidence again because I've lost it again.

I don't know but put my name down [in this book] as "Nissah". N-I-S-S-A-H. Because it means "woman".[3]

---

3 Surah An-Nisa is a chapter in the Quran.

DEALING WITH IT

I'm on the path to healing again. I was in such denial. I've been in denial for a long time but I do not think that I've forgiven my [oldest] brother and my mother. That's where I got stuck – because intellectually, I've given him so much power over my life, and also my mother.

I think having children has forced me to start dealing with it. I cannot keep shoving it aside, and also because it's taboo to speak about the dead. It's because of this taboo that abuse keeps happening. Nobody talks about it. That's why it continues.

I felt so alone because my mother was making me feel like a liar. I had so many arguments with her. I had so many fights when I gave birth and she was here for two months. One day, I'd be free with her, laughing and talking, and the next day, fighting. But it was the period that I needed to confront her.

I asked her one day, so if my brother was alive, you would have taken his side? She kept quiet as if she was saying "yes". She could not even give me that – because he's dead – to just say "no", to make me happy. She could have said, no, my child, I'd be on your side.

So I guess the healing is starting for me now. We are going to start therapy next year. Imran found a therapist. She seems to be helping him. We're going home for a month. We can start next year.

This year has been difficult. For me, it's been dark. I've been fighting myself.

I must start. It's one thing to preach to children but I truly believe that they learn more from your actions. They are always clued in. They are evolving creatures. They always pick up on what you're feeling.

ANGER AND FEAR

The other thing is that I have this anger management issue. I sometimes take it out on my children. I shout at them and Imran has been a great help to me.

I'm a bit scared because I'm finishing up my studies again. I do not have a career. I'm a bit of a realist, sometimes, a pessimist trying to be optimistic.

Imran and I have been married for 12 years now. I've always known that marriages are not for forever because I see lots of divorces. I've not seen it with my parents. I've always thought it's a 50-50 thing. With diplomats: they have one of the highest divorce rates. I've always had that fear at the back of my mind, with three children. I needed to figure out a plan B, C and D, especially since they've become accustomed to that kind of lifestyle.

When I go back home, it'll be a harsh reality. I do not want that for my children. They are studying at an international school. We went to a parents' workshop. They have such a brilliant way of teaching – they teach values, and leadership stuff and concentrate on awesome life themes. I am in awe of them. It's like taking a hundred steps backwards when we go home. I'm praying that when we go back, we'll be able to handle it and continue with a good schooling system.

NOT MY FAULT

The first thing I learnt was, it was not my fault.

I'd look at my daughter; she's six years old. And I'd tell myself: it was not my fault. That you were not a slut. As many times as I had said that, it still did not sink in with me.

If I felt pleasure, it was a natural reaction because it's the way your body works. It's not about you, it was about the other person. And for me, I'm learning something new, from our conversation about forgiveness. I think it's OK to accept what had happened but I tried to forgive. It was not truthful, it was not honest.

I really wish that victims would not lose their power because it messes things up for a long time. Intellectually, I tried dealing with it but it keeps coming up in my marriage, and with my children, if I don't deal with it.

I wish that victims will be just survivors, and not give power to their abusers. *I do not want to live in the darkness.*

You want to be free. You want to be you.

This is the strange thing as I know talking about it heals but maybe when my brother died, my mother talked and talked about it, and I was silent. I had no voice. My mom said, yes, you must talk, you must deal with it. She was the only one that healed. And I think that's why I kept quiet because my mother talked and talked so much about him. Even when I tried to be a good child for her, I never really spoke about this. I knew, it's one thing to intellectualise, it's another thing not to react, to move on.

I think that messed me up for a long time. It's the little things that I did myself. My daughter asks me, "Who taught you to cook?" My mother never taught me to cook. I learnt by watching her and by watching other people. I used to take the good qualities of other people to learn and try to better myself.

I had an aunt who was very poised and very rich, and I used to watch her as well. I used to learn from the other women around me in my life. My mother never taught me to drive. She never taught me when I got my period. I freaked out. The "birds and bees" talk, she gave me when I was about seven or eight. She called me into a room: "A woman is like a flower, the man is like a watering can. He waters her and she blooms."

I was confused, this was her way to talk about sex, basically! I learnt everything else on TV.

BREAKING THE SILENCE

Imran asked me, are you going to be honest with your children? Yes. I do not know at which point to tell them my story. I do not want to tell them and do more harm than good. I need to protect them from all that so that they can have a relationship with my mother. And I do not want them to have any ill feelings towards her. She's old enough. What if she dies? Would that do any good? Eventually, I do want my children to learn the truth, maybe not now, but later.

There's a part of me that's become so silent for so long because I don't believe in feeling sorry for myself. If I say I want to do something, I want to do it. I do not want to talk about something unless I know I'll do something about it. I don't want to be "that way". Be that "downer", say "sorry, I am going through this" while processing the experience.

I was saying to Imran, "Do I use my name for this story?" For him, I have to use my name and I need to own it now. This then becomes my story, I will give it a voice.

There's a part of me – I was telling Imran – my story feels like another person's story. I'm grateful for the life I have now. I do not ever covet anyone else's life. I always look to somebody that's worse off. I always think: so what, Nissah? There are other people who have it worse. Now and then, I would feel despair or anger because of the abuse, but look at how much I have!

I'm almost scared to pop the bubble. I have three amazing children, I have a good husband and I'm scared in case it bursts. I want to be ready for that. As much as Imran assures me, saying he'd never cheat on me or abandon me, I'm realistic. Anything could happen to him and I'm sitting here with three children. I worry about that, which is why I'm concerned about making plans. There's a part of me that thinks: I'm 40 years old and I do not have a career.

TEMPTED FATE

This is the amazing part of my journey. I do not ever feel like I've had it so bad. I feel like I've experienced so much because I always feel that God was at my back. As much as I've tempted fate. I've put myself in situations that were dangerous – when it comes to drugs and alcohol. I was in "adventurous" situations. I've been there and I've gotten away with it.

It is about the choices I make once I make up my mind. Who am I? I'm insignificant, but it's also about other survivors.

When I did therapy the first time, my marriage was on the rocks; the therapist at the time introduced me to another woman who came from a similar background. I had never met this woman before, but she was a friend of a friend. It's a small community. I was drawn to this woman for some very strange reason. When I found out that we had a mutual friend, I felt relieved, almost. It was not just another face, we are all part of the same family.

I'm trying to finish up my degree. I think I failed one of my exams though so I might have to repeat it next year. I'm seriously thinking about what I need to do and looking at women's rights issues and non-governmental organisations, and women empowerment etc.

So I need to start finding my way. I've basically cut myself off from everyone.

I'll have to work to be independent. It's strange to find myself where I am now. It's not scary, it's my reality. I need to change that now, *insya' Allah*.[4]

FAMILY LIFE

We're really close – Imran and I – so we know exactly which buttons to push. So when we argue, we go deep. We go for the jugular. But at the same time, we look out for each other. It feels comfortable. I feel that we're starting to push each other. He's also pushing me. I think he's on his journey of accepting who he is and I can feel him not wanting to leave me behind.

I do not like to just talk about things so I need to push myself now. In the same breath, I do not regret spending time with the children. When I had my first child, she'd cry all the time, constantly. I could not imagine anybody else taking care of her. I could not imagine anyone else tolerating her crying.

---

4 "God willing" in Arabic.

Since then, I've appreciated the time with the children at home. I cannot imagine somebody else doing what I've gone through with them. I mean, I do get frustrated. I'm human.

RELEASE

But as they're growing now, I realise more and more that I need to start taking care of myself because you can't give when you have nothing to give. I *need* to start caring for myself.

I've always felt it'll be therapeutic once I talk. Like I said, it's the start.

The beginning of my release.

8

ARCHANA

31-year-old Archana was molested by her Sanskrit school teacher in Chennai, India. As a student, she reported the incidents to another teacher. While no action appeared to have been taken, the abuse stopped. In adulthood, she discovered that her sister was abused by the same teacher. Her sister, who had a borderline personality disorder, committed suicide in November 2012. Archana was also abused by various boyfriends. She is now a successful videographer and documentary maker, based in Delhi.

....

Au Bon Pain Café, Delhi
27th May 2015

MY SCHOOL

How old was I? I was in either class four or five – that's like when I was eleven or twelve… I'm not even sure. My school had a pinafore uniform until class five. And I was clearly not wearing a *salwar kameez*[1] so it must have happened in class five.

---

1 A *salwar kameez* is traditional Indian attire consisting of a long blouse and baggy pants.

Until class two, I was staying at my grandma's house which was one street away [from the school]. We were a joint family[2] then. Then we moved to a new place, a renovated apartment. The school and the apartment complex shared a compound.

The founder of the school – it was not the greatest of schools – was right next door. We had moved from Dubai during the Gulf War – it was 1991. My dad, a civil engineer, is the eldest of four children. My dad was the only one with kids; the rest were too young. The school principal and my grandmother were close friends. My grandfather had passed away before I was born. It was the middle of the school year so it was not easy to get into any other school in Chennai. So, everyone just decided to put me in that school.

In class three or four, we had to choose a third language. It was just for us to learn a new language, and we weren't really tested on it. My school was religious; it was mainly Hindu but we used to celebrate Christmas as well. So Sanskrit was offered to us as an additional language. There were no examinations; nobody took it seriously, not even the teachers.

MY TEACHER

The Sanskrit professor joined the school when I was in class three or something. Somehow I never really liked him. At that time, I just felt that he was being creepy. It was obvious that he was paying me undue attention. I was very fair and I thought that was the reason I got more attention from him.

I didn't like it when people complimented me for my fair skin because then, even if I get high marks, classmates or

---

2   A joint family is an extended family living under the same roof.

relatives would just say that was because I was fair-skinned.

This Sanskrit teacher would not really teach because it was not a serious subject and he was the only Sanskrit teacher. There were a lot of teachers teaching various subjects. If one person was doing a shit job of it, another teacher would have been able to catch it. But in this case – he was the only one teaching the subject. So nobody knew what he was up to.

Drawing by Archana

He'd just walk into class and ask us to start reading the textbook, and he'd call us, one at a time, to his table. It was not like he was teaching science or mathematics and it was not like I was a weak student. I was always the first or second rank holder. So I never understood why I was called to the table.

When he called me, obviously, the rest of the class could see. Nobody would look up; everyone would be reading their books. Everyone would think that I was doing it to get marks. And I was already the first rank holder and so nobody liked me in the first place!

The students could see me from the front and people – teachers and students – could see me from the side, as they walked by in the corridor when I was called to his table. I remember that this happened most of the time. A class of 40 students would have maybe 15 girls, and the rest would be boys. So there was not a large number of girls to begin with. I don't know whether he was looking for any particular features in me or any other girl. Perhaps it was only fair girls?

He was fair himself. A lot of Tam-Brahms[3] are. I don't know what his intention was for him to pick me. The first few times I was called, I was distant and trying to figure out what he was trying to say. I just remember that there was nothing of importance. Both of us – me and him – knew it was just pretence.

I had no idea what abuse was, nobody told me. So I had no idea.

What he used to do – while I was reading or underlining words in my textbook or whatever – he used to put his hand up my skirt from behind. I am sure my other classmates could totally see it, unless they were blind! He might have thought that nobody saw it but I'm pretty sure they did.

I remember the boys giggling but I never made eye contact with anybody at those times even though people were right in front of us. Because I knew that the moment I saw someone looking at me, my whole image would fall apart.

SHUTTING OFF

I remember shutting everybody off so when people called my name, I wouldn't hear them. I was afraid people like my seniors, my sister or her classmates would see me standing there in front of the class, with his hand up my skirt. I knew a lot of people in that school. And my family was literally friends with the principal's family and people knew people, and that, for me, was stressful.

And I was scared that my family would come to know about what's happening and I didn't want that even though it

---

3 Short form for Tamil-Brahmins. Brahmins comprise the highest caste in the Hindu caste system.

should have been the other way round. I didn't want anybody to know, least of all my family.

I was also scared that I might lose my friends if they came to know about this. He used to put his hands up my skirt, pull my underwear down and put his finger in. But he'd start slow. First, he'd put his hand on the thigh. If somebody were to walk past, he'd freeze, or even take his hand out. If that happened, he'd have to start again on the thigh, and slowly work his way up.

IT WENT ON

He must have thought, "If I do it really slowly, nobody would know." For me, that was stressful but also a *blessing*. When there were interruptions, he would stop and then he'd start all over again. So I hoped that it would get interrupted… and a couple of times, it was. This went on maybe one entire school year. I would avoid him at every occasion. But there was no reason why I could not go to class.

At that point in the 1990s, there was no option to bunk a class. We were terrified of doing such a thing. But there was the "Annual Day" every year and I'd sign up for a dance, a play, or anything, and hence the rehearsals would take me out of classes.

I don't know how long this went on. A couple of times, I tried to be rude to him. I thought it was the only way. I couldn't confront him on this. I thought if I was a bit disrespectful in class and snap at him, I thought he'd get the message. But instead he'd snap back and I was scared that he'd tell someone… which was strange because he should have been the one who was scared.

TAMIL-BRAHMINS

Tam-Brahms have two sects – one is Iyer and the other is Iyengar. They usually didn't even inter-marry in those days. I'm an Iyer. Iyengars – in those days – you can spot them. They'd wear the *naamam* on their forehead.

A guy in my class would paint this on his forehead. I used to tease him: where did you find the time to do this in the morning, I'd ask. Because he'd have to dip a stick in white colouring, paint the "U" on his forehead, and paint the orange bit on. He'd have to mix the coloured powder with water to make the paint. I'm guessing it would take at least 10-12 minutes. I barely even had time to take a bath on a school day. I would not even put on shoe polish, for lack of time.

This guy would always be the second-rank holder. I was usually the first-rank holder. He used to be my competitor – or at least that was how his mom saw it. She was a tall, dominating and loud woman. She'd talk very nicely to me but I knew all she wanted were my class notes. She was looking for something magical in those notes that would make her son score more! But I had nothing in my notes.

Both the Sanskrit professor and this second-rank holder were Iyengars and they would chat and bond so much during and after school. I had mixed feelings about this because this classmate was a good friend of mine but I hated him being friends with the guy I loathed. I'd meet him after school, and he would be chatting with the teacher. I didn't want to be talking to the teacher, so I'd avoid him. That was a confusing situation.

THE NEIGHBOURHOOD

The Sanskrit teacher used to live in my neighbourhood.
And this classmate too. This Sanskrit teacher probably lived
a few minutes away from my house. I remember being
uncomfortable: there were times when I was out cycling – I
would wonder what would happen if this guy walked up to
me? What if I was wearing a dress or something? I did not
want him intruding into my personal space. I didn't want
him to meet or see any of my friends and family members.

I remember once walking down the street with my mother
and coming across the guy. There was no way to ignore him
as he was right across us. So he came up and spoke to me and
I remember feeling protective of my mother because I felt
that this guy was so creepy and that he should not be allowed
to speak to my mother who had no idea who he actually
was. I remember wanting to end the conversation as quickly
as I could. I remember pulling her and I wonder what my
mother must have thought about it.

It was a little awkward but it was OK. The thing about
my mom is that we are not confrontational at all. We don't
really talk and sort things out, we'd just let things simmer on
its own. It'd be simpler to just say, "Listen, this is shit and not
cool and all." But I never had the balls to do that.

KEEPING BOUNDARIES

After that, I remember being really, really awkward about
him. I wanted to keep the interactions with him to a bare
minimum. If I couldn't avoid him at Sanskrit class, then I
tried hard to make sure that's the only place I saw him and

nowhere else. So I spent a lot of time just trying to avoid him. If he was going to be at an event, I would not be there. Probably this was when I started filling up my entire schedule with lots of activities.

I don't feel unfair about blaming him for everything that's turned out bad in my life though. Even if it's not true, I don't mind. I don't know how to be nice to him.

BEING BRAHMIN

He was definitely single. He was young, in his late twenties, perhaps. He was skinny and fair. I don't know what he studied. He probably had studied the Vedas.[4] He probably took pride in being a Tam-Brahm. He probably would not have talked to non-Brahmins. We were from a very Brahmin neighbourhood and our school was very Brahmin even though we had the Christmas holiday, and we had Christian songs along with Hindu songs in our morning prayers.

He came from South Chennai. The neighbourhood we were in was predominantly Brahmin because every third house had a Brahmin family living in it. The people we saw in public, our school and socio-economic circles, were all upper-caste and Brahmin. Brahmins mixing with Brahmins. Probably now that I think about it, I probably only met the Brahmins because of my family. Back then, the divide was real: Brahmins and non-Brahmins. The Brahmin families would often identify others as "non-Brahmins". They were conditioned to think that Brahmins were the best. Now, you could be jailed for saying something like that.

---

4 The Vedas are an ancient body of texts comprising poetry and hymns, the latter forming Hindu scripture.

It was frowned upon to say something like that in school because school was supposed to be an equaliser – you were not supposed to differentiate. But there were undercurrents. There was a tailor in the neighbourhood – we would talk to his daughter but we would not be friends with her, because of the class difference. There were all these undercurrents that the kids would pick up from our family's influence. There was a whole Brahmanical way of life.

At my grandmother's house, my grandmother was very staunch – the maid could not enter the kitchen. After the crockery and utensils have been washed by the maid, my grandmother would pour a bucket of water over them before one of the daughters-in-law brings them inside. Once you've poured water, family members could touch them. At first, I did not understand – I thought the maid and all domestic help were dirty people. Then I started to know what the fuck happened then. But we barely had the education then to tell the difference between right and wrong. At that time, everyone took it [the caste rules] at face value.

This teacher was supposed to have learnt all about the Vedas. He was a very proud Brahmin. He was mostly talking to the Brahmin boys. They would mostly talk about religion and the Vedas. And I found it repulsive simply because I didn't like him and I didn't like what he stood for. So I found the Vedas etc at the time repulsive. I thought that if he studied the Vedas and he turned out to be such a crappy human being, then the scriptures must be crappy.

BEING BUSY

I started filling up my days – I took up Bhagavad Gita[5] classes. The Gita had nothing to do with the Vedas – it was in the Mahabharata, about the rules of law. About *dharma*,[6] basically. I do not remember jack shit.

I was just deluding myself into trying to understand the Gita but I clearly didn't. I was average at a lot of things. I didn't know what I was good at. Maybe somebody needed to tell me.

I used to attend Bharatanatyam[7] classes religiously. The dance teacher used to come to my house. I thought I was good at it but I never performed in front of anybody. But that was because the teacher was old school and he believed that a student is ready for the world to see only when he or she is absolutely perfect.

I learnt the dance form for eight to 10 years. In the evenings, I would dance. My sister also learnt classical Carnatic singing. I was not good at it but I wanted to try. I used to go for music classes as well, and just sit there. I did sports, pottery, dancing, singing, painting, Hindi classes. I felt I had to engage myself and be busy all the time and be really good at everything. My parents were not pushing me into doing these things. I was signing up for all these classes on my own.

I'd call up the dance teacher myself and arrange for him to come to my home to teach. I would make sure that my parents were okay to pay the fees required. I figured it was easier to do things myself instead of relying on my busy parents, so I started doing things on my own. I would say to

---

5   The Bhagavad Gita is Hindu scripture that forms part of the Hindu epic, the *Mahabharata*.
6   Fate.
7   The Bharatanatyam is a major classical Indian dance form.

my parents, "Would you be OK to spend 200 rupees on this thing?" And when they said yes, I'd sign up.

I worried about money and I didn't want to ask my parents. I did small things – part-time jobs, freelance writing, cheerleading – to make some extra cash. I saved up money for stuff like French classes and travel. My dad was working; he did not have his own company then. I was extremely mindful of what I was spending on. I did not spend money on food, clothes or even movies. I can't imagine now, passing up on movies!

Back then, I had to ask my parents to take me anywhere, because they wouldn't let me go anywhere on my own. They would constantly worry about my safety. They wouldn't even let me do certain sports because it was "risky". They sort of ruined me because I can never really do adventure sports like rafting or climbing without thinking about different ways I could die doing this. So I am conditioned into thinking I am not fit to do these things and that something terrible is going to happen to me. Even now, I don't tell my parents everything that I've done, because they will worry about it even after it's over. If I told them I went bungee jumping, my mom would freak out saying, "Oh, my God, what if you had gotten hurt? Why did you do it?"

TELLING

I don't know when the abuse stopped. I remember telling my class teacher – I made up a lame reason to see her after school. During school hours, there'd be the other kids. So I would not have a moment with her alone. I could not make up an excuse to talk to her privately. It was too risky. What if I fumbled and everybody came to know?

So, I just waited one day after school, pretending to catch up on my notes, and sat there until every last person walked out of class, but the teacher was still there. Thinking back, it must have taken me a few days or weeks of trying to find the perfect opportunity like that because, it's very rare to find yourself alone with the teacher in an empty classroom. There are always too many people.

She was Christian. I don't remember her name, though. She was very straightforward. I had been putting off telling her about the abuse because I was constantly afraid that she was not going to believe me, and worse, she might think I was the one responsible for this.

So I told her and she was surprised, but there was really no dramatic reaction from her side. Maybe that left me a little confused. Maybe it wasn't such a big deal and I made a big deal out of it. Drama Queen. I felt it was my fault that the abuse happened. I didn't understand my place in society. Like I do not understand the place of something like that [the abuse] in society. Maybe that's what adults did, and I just wasn't intelligent enough to know that yet. I was an overprotected 10-year-old who didn't know the first thing about abuse, or anything for that matter.

I didn't know it was abuse. I just knew that your private parts were private. They were not to be talked about. There was also the fact that he was religious and who preached and he must therefore be somebody who was completely right. We were always told to obey elders. We were told NOT to question authority.

Parents were of two kinds – one kind that would stand up and defend their children EVEN if they were wrong, and the other kind who would apologise on behalf of the kids and punish the kids EVEN if they were not entirely wrong. My parents were the second kind. They would ALWAYS, ALWAYS make sure we were "corrected" and not society. I think their intention was not to bother anybody else. But to me, it meant: "Whatever bad happens, YOU are responsible."

When I told my teacher about the abuse, I don't know how many details I gave her – where he was touching me etc. I'd probably told her he had put his finger in my underwear and I left it to her to fill in the blanks.

After telling my teacher, I don't know what happened. But this guy was not fired. I never experienced anything with him again. It didn't become public and I was thankful for that. But I'm surprised that nobody took any action. But I think my teacher made sure that I didn't have to attend his classes. I'm not sure whether I got some mental closure then. I remember this female teacher did something good but I can't remember what, but at least she didn't make me feel bad for reporting the abuse.

The Sanskrit teacher never bothered me again. I don't know whether it was because she told him. I was worried that he might talk to my family and tell everyone to take revenge. So I would compulsively avoid eye contact with him. But there was this understanding that I had gotten the message across to him that what he did wasn't right. Although I didn't confront him, he came to understand that and we just avoided each other.

BEING BLAMED

I still didn't know much about abuse. I just cringed when it happened, again and again. I didn't want anybody to find out. My reaction to every situation of abuse was: if I freeze and don't scream, then nobody would come to know. That was very important – that nobody should know. I'd been groped in temples. Even when my parents were around, people have touched me. Men have brushed their private parts against me and I don't think anybody other than me and the abuser knew about these things.

My ex-boyfriends would try to make their advances in a very obvious way – after we'd broken up – and I was just afraid of telling anybody because everyone would just blame me. Society was like that: if you were ready to go out with someone, then it's sort of on you. But now, victim-blaming has become a major issue.

Once, I was groped. My mother and aunt were there with me in Pondicherry but I didn't say anything. Another time, someone was following me on my bike very closely. I was buying food for my family and I just went into the restaurant and looked through the window, waiting for the stalker to leave. He was standing near my bike, I didn't see what he was doing. When I couldn't see him there anymore, I walked out to get my bike and leave, and then when I touched the handlebars of my scooter, it was covered with... He had jerked off right there.

I didn't tell anybody. I came back home and pretended everything was normal. It was too gross for me to tell anyone.

Then there was an ex-boyfriend whom I met on New Year's Eve. I went to my school friend's house after partying with my sister, her boyfriend and some friends. Two of my ex-boyfriends were there. I wasn't worried because I thought we were all friends who have moved past any bitter feelings.

One of them tried to rape me that night. My friends were in the other room. Then this guy said, "You have to have sex with me right now." I was afraid that he would break something on my head and kill me. This guy hurt me physically.

I could have called out and my friends would have come to help. But I was so afraid that maybe I would be blamed. That maybe, they would take his side.

At that point of time, in society, girls did not date men openly – you're supposed to pretend you have not had sex in your life, and you don't intend to do so. That happens a lot in the Tam-Brahm community.

So again, I didn't tell anyone, but this time, I spoke up. I said to him, "If you don't stop now; I'd scream and you'd be kicked out of the house." I literally had to fight my way out of that room.

And then I had to go join my friends in the next room pretending that nothing had happened and that we were just talking to each other. I didn't want to create a fuss so I stayed in the house. I couldn't go back to my own house. My parents would not let me go out late in the night unless it was a sleepover at a girlfriend's. And I was probably drunk. There was no way to justify my turning up at their doorstep at 3am. I probably had told them that I was sleeping over at a girl's house.

The same night, this other guy whom I had briefly dated in high school also tried to take advantage of me. But I just lay there pretending to sleep and praying that he would just leave me alone. That was the worst night of my life!

After that night, I'd reached the conclusion that the reason I was getting abused over and over again was because I never spoke up. Right from the teacher who came from a position of power, to all the others.

I still know those people – the ex-boyfriends. We have mutual friends. I would not meet them alone, or pick up their calls or call them. But if they were there with my friends, I'd say hello.

But assholes are assholes. It took me 29 years to say that!

Starbucks, Delhi
31st May 2015

RELATIONSHIPS

After that New Year's night, I left early in the morning as soon as the sun came out.

I told my boyfriend everything about the two ex-boyfriends and how one was violent and trying to rape me, and the other was silently pushing his body against mine in the dead of the night. He was saying, "What the hell's wrong with you? Why didn't you say anything?"

I said I couldn't because I thought I would be blamed for whatever that had happened. He got a bit annoyed because I kept going back to the same pattern where I'd just freeze when something bad happened. He said that unless I started somewhere, I'd never speak up. We had a long conversation where he said that I should speak up when something happens, not after. I don't know if this was before or after telling him about my Sanskrit teacher. I think it was after. By that time, he already knew about these other stories and he could see a pattern.

I've been conditioned into thinking that everything I do was my fault – because I was there in the first place, and it was my actions in the past. Which is why to this day, I don't confront anybody if I'm angry. If I feel there's even the slightest mistake on my part, I feel I probably deserved it.

Outside of relationships, I'm still bound by the social courtesies. If I'm at work, if somebody was throwing their weight around or there were people trying to get me to do their work for them – even though I can see they are trying to take advantage of me, I would still do it. Because I hate being in an argument or a tense situation. It would ruin that one particular relationship for me permanently. Imagine walking into office everyday and looking at this colleague every single day. One fight could ruin the rest of the working days for me. Because at the end of the day, I go back to a different set of people. The people at home are those who matter to me. I can smile and get through a day at work even if I don't like them.

But at home, it's a relationship. I feel the need to explain every point when I'm annoyed. I might not say it right then, but I would explain later why it was pissing me off. And I'd only say I am "controlling" because I feel sometimes that I make better decisions when it comes to certain things. When I'm certain about certain subjects or territories, I'd do it because I don't trust other people to do it correctly, and by that, I mean doing it my way. That's when I get controlling. I know I have to be more trusting of other people.

MY SISTER

My sister and I grew up together. We shared a room. She moved out earlier than me. She and I were two and a half years apart in age, but academically, that was two years. Like, when I was in class seven, she was in class nine. So when she finished her third year of college, I had finished the first year. That's when she went to a different state to do her Masters and I was still in second year of my undergrad. I remember I used to visit her every summer and we used to backpack and travel to many places.

Once, we were just sitting around and talking. It started with her talking about a guy who was a moron. We started discussing about how there were a lot of morons. We started telling stories. She told me about this guy who molested her or something of that sort and I told her how I was groped in temples and felt up on buses. I was telling her things that had happened to me – crazy stalkers, gropers, cat callers, the works. It was almost like a competition – each story that we shared was worse than the previous one. And at one point, I started narrating the entire episode about this Sanskrit teacher who would put his hands up my skirt. She was so surprised when she heard my story because she said the exact same thing happened to her. We were literally finishing each other's sentences.

We were both shocked. She had gone through the exact same thing. I asked her, "Would he call you to the front of the class?" She replied, "Yes".

"And does he make you read out some random shit?" I probed further. And she said, "Yeah".

It suddenly hit home and we thought, "Shit!" She had not reported it to anyone. I told her that I did and she was surprised. We laughed about it maybe because we were not used to discussing such heavy topics back then. I had told my husband, who was at that time my boyfriend, about the discussion with my sister. He was completely surprised that no one took any action.

FINDING OUT MORE

I never asked her again. I wanted to know more about this but I don't know why we did not talk. We just got talking about other things. We probably just stopped because maybe we were a little emotional. We didn't continue and we didn't have anything more to say.

I remember telling my boyfriend, "You'd never believe what just happened." He was also shocked that we both went through abuse by the same guy in school. I was so angry with this teacher that he had done the same thing to my sister as well. I was probably angrier about him abusing my sister than about me. I had so much anger that I couldn't do anything about it. Because it happened so early in my life. And I couldn't even trace him without having to reveal why I was chasing him in the first place.

That Iyengar guy in my class would probably be the only one who'd remember. There was this other guy whom I used to go to school with – they were both very good friends. I wasn't in touch with these two guys, not even on Facebook. Other people in my class sent me Facebook friend requests, but I did not accept them. This was six to eight years back when Facebook was really popular. From that school, I think I have very few people on my Facebook. There's nobody I'm in touch now to whom I could ask about the teacher. I'm talking about 21 years ago. They must all be 29 years by now. They might still be in touch with one another.

These same two guys – I bumped into them at a mall eight years ago. The last time we saw each other, we were really small – it was strange to see everyone all adult, with moustaches. I was very, very shaken after that meeting. It just brought up the memory of those days. Over the following couple of weeks, I was debating whether I should ask them about the Sanksrit teacher. If they knew where he was. The abuse still wasn't that old at that point – it was still a lot fresher than now. But I did not have the balls to ask them. I had the feeling that they sort of liked him.

A couple of years back, I wanted to make a series of videos about people who had been abused and who had never confronted their abusers. I thought we could go back and track the abusers down and sometimes am sure they would be right there in their family. I thought of having a video of the confrontation between the survivor and the abuser – to see whether the latter would deny it. If you asked them whether they did it, what would be their answer? But of course, I never did the series.

DEALING WITH ABUSE

My hometown was a small city. I've never spoken about my abuse to anybody from my city. I've spoken to a couple of girls in Delhi and now, I feel OK talking about it. I'm still wary of calling myself a survivor of child sexual abuse.

But now if I sense that if anyone was being abusive to

me, I'd walk away. If somebody was teasing me on the road, I'd make sure I'd make noise or chase them. I'm no longer ashamed to call out these people. Most women, they think, there's the off chance that this guy didn't mean it. So most women are really nice people and that's why we let the abusers get away.

That's what happens to me. Why should I raise my voice? What if it was a general mistake?

If you take public transport, you'll see a lot of things. There'd be some men who are doing something. You can call it unintentional and move on, or you'd have to tell them, convey to them, that it's not OK. In India, you'd have to constantly put up a tough exterior so as to convey that it's not OK to approach you.

ON BEING IN A RELATIONSHIP

The place I come from is super conservative. You can't date someone and then move on. If you fall in love with someone – they'd call it "love" – you'll have to get married. There's no concept of taking a relationship for the intrinsic values of having a relationship. You go in with the idea of marrying them.

Which was why if I felt any guy was ever getting clingy, I'd just break up. At that point, I just wasn't ready to be with anybody on a long-term basis. I felt that the moment you got committed, then the control thing begins. The moment you get into the whole commitment thing, you've given them power – anyway, that's what I thought – a whole game of power, to be used and be abused.

I was extremely commitment-phobic. I couldn't imagine being with one person, yet. It was not as if I would date everyone, I just saw everyone as weak. I didn't think men were strong at all. They were really weak.

I then became a different person dealing with abuse. I went through a phase trying to convince myself not to freeze.

STANDING UP FOR MYSELF

I remember taking the only train or bus to a small town in Karnataka because my sister was going through a bad breakup and I thought I should be there by her side. I didn't have enough money on me. I lied to my parents – I told them I was travelling for a college project.

I was in a bus and I was really exhausted after travelling for almost an entire day. There was this guy sitting behind me on the bus. I was falling asleep. He put his hand in between the seats, groping me. Some old woman was next to me. There was so much going on in my head. I finally snapped at him, "What are you doing?"

This was the first time I had done this – directly confront an abuser – and I felt happy that I had stood up for myself. I thought if I made a scene, then maybe other people in the bus would question him or even better, throw him out of the bus. But nothing. Nobody even bothered.

This woman next to me asked me, "What happened?" And I told her this old man just groped me. She replied, "OK." That's it. She just literally wanted to know what happened and she went back to sleep. India's not the place for women at all.

I could not do anything in the bus. I was there, and he was there. He did this thrice. The first two times, I was not sure what was happening, and then the third time, I gave it some thought – this is stupid; nobody would do this by mistake. So I yelled at this guy the third time he did it.

When I figured that the people in the bus didn't care at all, I just waited for the bus to reach the destination, so I could get off. We had reached a bus stop. I think we had to transfer to another bus. I got down. He did too. Suddenly, I started going crazy. I screamed at him like a mad person, "What did you think you were doing?" I screamed repeatedly before throwing an empty water bottle at him which I just picked up from the ground.

People just watched. They were just curious – they were watching because there was nothing else to do. There was no support – they were just curious onlookers. But at least, it was better that there were at least those onlookers. Had it been a deserted place, I could have gotten hurt.

Abuse that's happening in plain sight.

That was probably the first time I stood up for myself. In Delhi, people are aggressive. Women scream and shout all the time. The first roommate I had – she was wearing shorts and walking in a market in Noida [the capital of the state of Uttar Pradesh]. We were shopping for stuff for the house. We had hardly met but we got on really well. A guy groped her behind that day in the market. And she raised her voice, caught him by the collar, shook him up, called the cops and made him apologise. A big crowd had gathered.

I stood there and thought, "Wow, this woman is amazing. I would have never been able to do this."

That was a big lesson. Her point was, unless you embarrass him like that, he isn't going to stop himself from doing this to other women.

After that, I was very alert. Many times when people brushed past me, or they "accidentally" touch me in the wrong places, it would take me a few minutes to figure it out. I am always on "abuse alert". I notice who is on the street and who is coming near me, all the time. I spent a lot of days just chasing people who would "accidentally" grope me or brush past me. Sometimes, the onlookers are helpful.

Once, a guy brushed past me. I ignored it for three seconds, then I thought – the road was empty, he could have walked a kilometre away from me – the fucking road was empty. So I turned back and started walking towards him, faster than him. He started running and I was chasing him. This was in a Delhi Development Authority (DDA) colony, so there were many corners and turns. I would ask everyone, "You've seen this guy? He was wearing a blue shirt."

They'd ask me back, "Did he steal something?" And I said no, he touched me. People's reaction were: "It's OK, it's fine. He's not stealing from you." I thought: fuck this, and I ran and ran. I remember it being a hot summer's day.

CLOSURE

I couldn't find him. See, I never had closure. I never could get hold of an abuser, to just shake him and yell at him for what he did. There's so much accumulated anger in me. There's so much pent-up anger in me from all the past transgressions –

I might channel all of this at someone if they were to harass me. It must not be fair that all anger would be on this one person. But I don't care. I need to let go of it at some point but I just cannot. It's so hard to do that.

And now I don't think that I can ever... I mean, there's probably a lot of aggression left in me. But I think it's too late. I cannot confront this abuser or anybody else – people I've known or the unknown people. I cannot go back to these men now. They probably think that I do not remember.

Another incident I remember was when I was really young, in my apartment complex. There was this guy who was a plumber or an electrician. He was very nice to me. I don't know whether it was flirting or not. I'd be very wary of people who were very nice to me and I'd snap at them. A friend of mine, who was my peer, looked at me and said, "You shouldn't do shit like that. Then nobody would talk to you."

I wasn't even being mean. I just didn't want the attention. Ever since then, I could never make up my mind – should I be mean to people before they become mean to me? All these confusing things in my mind. I never tied all these things to being abused.

BEING TOUCHED

All through growing up, I used to get my cheeks pinched all the time. I used to hate that. That's what people do to kids, right? I was like, why were they touching me? Maybe that's why even now, I tend to over-think and over-analyse every situation. Are they touching me because of genuine affection or is it something else? This is sometimes a good thing, but it's *exhausting*.

I didn't like to be touched by women either. I didn't like to be touched at all. Now, of course, I've moved beyond that. And now I'm not that young anymore so I don't attract any of these abusers but that also means I cannot get my revenge or vent my anger and have my closure.

Probably at some point, I might find the name of this teacher. I still keep Googling him viz. "Sanskrit teacher in Chennai". But he could have moved away. Or he might even be dead! I hope he's not dead. I just want to ask him, "What the fuck were you thinking?"

I used to have these fantasies of finding his wife and being really mean and telling everyone, so that his kids would hate him, his wife would leave him and his parents would disown him. Like even if he was repenting by force, by making his family go against him – in my imagination, this is what would happen. In my fantasy, I want to ruin his happiness.

Anyway, none of this will happen.

MY SISTER'S DEATH

I don't know [if my sister's death in November 2012 was related to the abuser]. I've thought about it: maybe this was where it all started, she became a borderline, she started having trust issues. I was looking for a very simple answer. If it pointed to this guy, I'd find him. If I knew for sure, I'd make the trip back over and shamelessly ask everyone. I wouldn't have cared.

I've spoken to people she dated, her husband. Nobody seems to know. It's just me trying to look for closure. That I can close both chapters of our lives at one go. It's just very convenient for me. Maybe it could be. Maybe it couldn't.

I even asked my therapist. What he told me was, "You're just looking for a simple answer and sometimes the answers aren't that simple. You can't blame everything on one thing."

She's written about a lot of stuff in the past – there's this blog of hers, but not about what happened to her. I knew her Gmail password – she hadn't changed it in 10 years. One random day, after she passed away, I went through her inbox. I got really obsessed; I typed in keywords.

But I ended up reading about our conversations – me and her. That time when we talked about our abuse, it was not on Gchat as we were at home. So there was no record of it. She had changed her Gmail account several times. She was very careful about keeping records of anything. I think she deleted her personal stuff. Some of the conversations told me that she had been through something bad but she had never told anybody that I know. I was just going crazy because I was looking for an answer.

I wanted closure.

I'm very convinced she went through some shit of her own from whatever few pieces that I picked up. Borderline's a personality disorder. It's one of the lesser known ones. I'm sure a lot of people have it but haven't been diagnosed. The main thing is suicidal tendencies: it could be from trauma or it could be genetic. The reason no one really knows.

Even if somebody in my family has had a mental disorder, we wouldn't know it because nobody gets their mental health checked here. Even if someone has any mental issues, they just go to a temple because they assume that evil spirits have taken over the body.

It's complicated with her. The reason why she did what she did could have been anything. I've not investigated too much because it's just too much time and energy. But the reason why I had to find this teacher: I wanted to make him feel guilty. If you tell someone that he was responsible for somebody's death, that should hit you, right? Just to make him – I don't know – feel really bad.

I don't think I've spoken about it. I have spoken about it to a guy but we're no longer in touch, and also to my therapist. Now that it's been three years since the death, I've been able to handle it. My therapy also helps. Not just with this… I'm not looking for answers anymore. It's just peaceful. Stuff like this is too chaotic. To just let go, and knowing that the answers aren't all that simple, and you're fine with that. It's better than to work with nothing. But it's frustrating because I can't obsess about this all the time. I have other things to do.

HEALING

I've realised that the whole abuse affected me. It's taken me 15-16 years to figure that out. Maybe because of these issues, I don't like to hug. I don't hug enough, only those I've hugged before. I've never thought of dealing with this.

I still don't understand how the healing process works. I just know that the abuse is affecting me and my reactions – I still don't like being touched in many places. It is hard to explain to another person. We both might be very comfortable but still, there's this thing. It's not something that you can snap out of.

Now I'm not ashamed of that anymore because for the longest time, I couldn't tell anybody. I couldn't have forgotten it, obviously.

I was in denial: I told myself nothing had happened. Maybe I was ashamed. It was embarrassing to talk about; there was nobody I could talk to about it. There was no outlet. My husband – back then, he was my boyfriend – was the first person I was comfortable enough with whom I could talk to about these things. It was also the big reason why we got together as I also wasn't comfortable talking about this to anyone else.

So yeah, I'm still trying to understand the healing process. I've downloaded books on healing on my Kindle. With my therapist, I have not talked about my abuse too much because there are so many issues we are discussing about, and this doesn't take much of our time. I feel like right now, it'd take me a billion years… There's so many things at one go, like the thing with my sister, my relationship with my husband, and the abuse. The sessions are about the everyday issues; there's not even time to talk about the abuse.

Where this thing is going is: a lot of my behaviour and my problems come from my childhood, even before the abuse. I come from a Tam-Brahm family which instilled a lot of discipline so there was always this fear, as a child. There was a lack of space to express myself, being afraid of what I can or cannot say which probably was the reason why I could never really report any of those abuses that had happened at an early age.

The therapist can make a lot of connections with my past. He'd say, "Is this true because it could stem from your childhood?"

I'm really, really working at this but it's not like a syllabus where you can see what's ahead. Sometimes, I'm at step five but then I'd have to get back to step two. It *is* helping and some days, when there's so many things and I'm thrown into a session, I don't know where to begin.

The first eight to 10 sessions were very intense. I told my therapist that the day I could talk without all this intensity and sobbing, that would be the day when I'd say that we've been successful and I don't have to return. But the last two sessions were like that. And I'm still going to therapy. It's just that I'm trying to handle everything on my own.

For a long time, I thought therapy was for seriously damaged people. Going to a therapist would mean accepting that I was damaged. But I've realised now it's like going to the gym. The reason I went was that it was too confusing: was what was happening because of my abuse, or my DNA or from my childhood? It was too confusing to figure out on my own. I had so many questions and no answers and so many probabilities.

I thought I was depressed. I thought my perception was like those with schizophrenia, something of that sort. Then I figured that I just cannot manage all these questions in my head. That I'll have to put them in perspective by telling someone else what happened. Putting them into words – something as simple as that could help put things into perspective.

I'm slowly figuring things out. I'm fine talking about it openly with other people. Like casually mentioning that

I'm a survivor of child sexual abuse. If they cannot handle it, it's their problem. They might have problems asking me. That's fine and that's how society works, I guess. But I'm OK with it. I also think a lot of people have gone through this. The only way out is to have an easy conversation about it.

I have less anxiety. One good thing is: I am not looking for a miraculous recovery. I am not looking for a better version of me overnight. I was just focused on getting some balance. Just knowing that things cannot be perfect, not just me, but other people too. When you're talking about the past, you're also talking about other people's pasts and how my way of seeing it might conflict with that of the other person's. Like my parents, for example. My therapist would say, "Remember there are two perspectives and to not get carried away."

I had asked my therapist about borderline cases – could it have stemmed from child sexual abuse? Obviously he did not have a precise answer to that. He did not know my sister. There could have been something else big that nobody knew about that affected my sister. But he was right – and that calmed me – that there was no one simple answer to this.

I just wished I had known about abuse a lot earlier. I wished somebody had sat me down and explained these things to me. Ninety-nine percent of things we learn from experience, good and bad. How could you have learnt from this kind of experience? It's just exhausting.

I don't think that I'll go through something like this again unless there's a new pattern to abuse that I don't recognise. But I don't think so since I'm extremely paranoid and cautious. I'd look at a situation from all angles. I don't see how something like that would escape me now. Everything starts the same way and I think I can recognise the pattern.

9

DON

Don Ralfo was abused by his mother as a child. He is now in his sixties and lives in Hanover, Germany. He has retired because of his state of health and blogs about various issues including being a survivor of child sexual abuse (www.allespsychos.blogspot. de). He is married and has four adult children. This chapter is taken from a blog post by Don, translated from the German by Suhaila Gao.

....

MY FATHER

The sexual abuse started during my pre-adolescent years. Like every child, I loved sleeping with my parents in their big bed. My bed was in the same room as my parents' – which meant they could shuffle off the (usually unsolicited) guest back to his bed quickly.

I loved cuddling with my father upon waking up in the early mornings, begging him to tell me a story. I think there was a total of only two or three stories, and during the times when he was not feeling up to it, he would make up the shortest one he could think of. If I got too annoying, he would simply rub his stubble on my face – ensuring a speedy getaway on my part.

THE ABUSE

My father was a train driver and was often on the night shift. At times, he would be away for days. Whenever I was alone with my mother, I was allowed to sleep the entire night in their bed next to my mother. It was during one of these times that she consciously touched my genitals, stroking them tenderly. I did not think it to be unpleasant then as I had not known yet what sexual stimulation was.

With time, these "assaults" on my penis became a game between us. I would try to fend off the approaches but her hand would always slip back under the bedcovers to touch my sensitive parts. At some point, it became too much for me to handle. I did not really understand what was happening and I found the game tedious and boring. But my mother did not stop. It dragged on for years and when I hit puberty, the location of the scene changed from the bed to normal everyday settings.

I began to hit her fingers whenever they crept towards me during the day, her face sheepish. But she was in no way daunted and continued to grope me. One day, I got a recorder as a present and started taking music lessons in school. From then onwards, the recorder became my weapon. I would hit her hand with it during her assaults. But she still did not stop. At one point she got a huge bruise on her hand from my hitting it with the wooden recorder. She left me alone for quite a while after that.

At 14, I went on a holiday together with my mother to the Italian Riviera. We shared a double bed, of course. That was the first time that she made her move on me after a long period, and I became sexually aroused. On my part, I pressed myself against her body. I had been, by that point in time, "enlightened" and was sexually mature.

I would have had sexual intercourse with my mother at that time had she not gotten alarmed suddenly and withdrew from me. It is fortunate that we did not come to that point and since then, she has completely stopped from making her disgusting moves on me.

RELATING TO GIRLS

I, however, had serious problems in my youth when it came to having normal and healthy relationships with girls of my age. As I am neither a psychologist nor a psychiatrist, I cannot gauge how much this stems from my unhealthy relationship with my mother. In any case, the relations I had with the fairer sex were troubled ones characterised by excessive, exaggerated fears. I was not able to admit to a girl that I liked her even if she had made it clear that she fancied me.

When my first girlfriend asked me whether I wanted "to go steady" with her, I had a panic attack and was paralysed by fear. I asked her to give me some time to consider it even though I had wanted a girlfriend for quite a while by then because I never dared to approach a girl. When I told her I was in agreement, I was as stiff as a poker when she hugged and kissed me. I was in full panic mode about behaving stupidly or admitting my feelings. That died away only after a considerable amount of time.

INCEST

I know that at least two of my closest childhood friends have had similar experience with their mothers. One of them lived in the same apartment building.

I do not know how far their incestuous relationships went. It was, and remains, a taboo subject – one which we only very seldom broach and openly talk about. Back then as well as today, mothers are somehow sacrosanct and have a default invisible halo. No one dares to pin sexual assault on women.

DOMESTIC VIOLENCE

In the eyes of the public, sexual assault is purely the domain of men and since the women's liberation movement in 1968, it has remained a hot topic in the media. Women's shelters sprouted and men have been stigmatised as violent, penis-driven oppressors of women. Studies on domestic violence with women as the perpetrators do not get the public's attention at all because neither the government nor the media picks up on them. The taboo topic simply does not fit in with the worldview.

I would very much like to know how many other boys have been sexually harassed and traumatised by their mothers and other women during their childhood. If within my immediate circle, there are already two cases of it excluding my own, I am certain that there are many others which have gone unreported or been hushed up. It is entirely possible that such cases have contributed in some part to male violence against women and other male psychological disorders.

Psalm eines Depressiven
May 2009

Ich bin wütend!
Wütend auf mich und wütend auf Gott.
Wütend auf mich, weil ich mich nicht ändern kann.
Wütend auf Gott, weil er mich nicht heilt und ich weiter
*   an mir leiden muß.*

Wozu dieses sinnlose Leid?

Wozu die ständige Hoffnung auf ein Morgen, wenn sich
*   doch nichts ändert?*

Ich wünschte ich könnte schlafen – ewig schlafen – doch ich
*   muß noch Meilen gehn, bevor ich ruhen kann.*
Gibt es ein Himmelreich? Dann komme bald, Herr Jesus.

Warum diese ständige Verzweiflung? Immer wiederkehrende
*   Belanglosigkeiten.*
Gibt es eine zukünftige Hölle, oder bin ich da schon längst?
Ich bin wie Sisyphos, der den Stein immerfort bergauf
*   rollt, aber nie die Spitze des Berges erreicht. Und immer*
*   wieder entgleitet er und rollt bergab.*

Ich kann nicht mehr und mag nicht mehr.
Macht mir keine neue Hoffnung, die doch nur wieder
enttäuscht wird.

Die schlimmste Hölle wäre, wenn es zu den Höllenstrafen
gehörte, an einen Erlöser zu glauben, der mich aus
der Hölle rettet, um mich dann in das ewige Feuer
zurückzuwerfen.
Immer und immer wieder.
Hoffnung auf Erlösung – die dann enttäuscht wird zu
ständig tiefer gehender Pein im Sumpf des Verderbens.

Das kann kein Gott der Liebe sein, der sich so etwas ersann!
Nein so etwas gibt es nicht.
Das ewig Böse ist undenkbar und unvorstellbar.
Kein Gott der Liebe würde so etwas zulassen. – Wo ihr
Wurm nicht stirbt und ihr Feuer nicht erlischt.

Psalm of a Depressive

translated from the German by Eirliani Abdul Rahman

I am angry!
Angry with myself and angry with God
Angry with myself, because I cannot change myself
Angry with God, because he has not healed me and I must
*   continue to suffer.*

What's the purpose of this senseless suffering?

What's the purpose of this ever hoping for a morning when
*   nothing changes itself?*

I wish I could sleep – sleep forever – but I must yet go for
*   miles before I lie in peace.*
Is there a Kingdom of Heaven? Then please come soon,
*   Mr. Jesus.*

What's the purpose of these continued doubts? Ever
*   returning vacuity.*
Is there a future Hell, or have I already long been there?

I am like Sisyphus, whose rock always rolls uphill reaches
*   the summit. And always, does the rock slip and roll*
*   downhill.*
I cannot anymore and do not want to anymore.
Do not give me hope that will only again disappoint.

The worst hell is, when one already belongs to these hellish
  stratosphere, to believe in a Redeemer, who will rescue me
  from Hell, just to throw me back into the eternal flames.
Over and over again.
Hope for redemption – that then disappoints – will bring
  me to ever deeper torment in the swamp of Debauchery.

That cannot be a God of Love, who schemes so!
No, there is nothing like that.
The permanent Evil is unthinkable and unimaginable.
No God of Love would have allowed that. Where its worm
  not die and where its fire is not extinguished.

10

LUCIE

23-year-old Lucie is half-English and half-Indonesian. As a child, she was abused by her gardener and her mother's co-worker. Her mother was also abused as a child. Lucie moved to Berlin at the age of 11, became pregnant at 15, and chose to keep the baby whom she named Silva. She is juggling her parenting responsibilities while working in Berlin. She is best friends with Nikita (see Chapter 11).

....

a letter
26th January 2015

Dear Lin,
My mother is Indonesian. Whenever we fight and I use a nasty tone of voice, she always reminds me: "*Nanti kalau kamau sudah punya anak dan dia ngomong sangat menyakitin, kamu bisa ngerasain.*" [Later when you get your own child and they talk back in a hurtful way, you'll feel it.]

My daughter is turning four in two weeks and those words are set on repeat in my head day after day. I'm scared of the pain that I gave to my mom.

I'm not particularly scared of my daughter using some sort of tone of voice with me as a teenager as long as she's honest with me. I'd rather see the dirty details instead of having it all sugar-coated. I'm scared of all the things I do not see, things that might happen behind my back.

My parents are really religious people. My dad's Christian and my mom is Muslim. They married because my mother got pregnant and so they felt it was their duty to marry. My father had to convert to Islam on the surface to win the blessings of my mother's parents, but later on he could not continue lying, and soon enough, everybody knew he was Christian. Both of them are very committed to their religions and have tried to convert the other, but I know that is going to be almost impossible.

My father has lived in Indonesia for a very long time, – approximately 20 years – and more or less adopted its culture. Despite their differences in beliefs, they share the same principles and one of those is no sex before marriage. Sex has always been such a taboo topic in our family. It's such a common Asian thing, I guess. In Indonesia, some girls cover their hair as soon as they start walking or going to school, depending on how strict the parents are. My mother was not so strict back then, she didn't wear a *hijab*[1] either and was pretty outgoing and accepting. However, she still preferred that we didn't walk around with our bellies showing or with too-short shorts, and we were never allowed to sleep over at a boy's house. She was very clear about that.

I have two younger siblings, one older half-brother and three older half-sisters, two of whom I have no contact with.

---

1 The hijab is a type of headdress worn by Muslim women.

My older brother was home-schooled. He went to school for the first time when he was 16, I think. He had a girlfriend for the first time when he started school. She was Australian and came over a lot. I was five or six when they were dating and only remember a few things about her.

What stuck in my head was a scene of my father banging on my brother's door, yelling her name and telling her to leave the house. My father had figured out that she had slept over without his consent. I hid behind the couch and my sisters were behind me; we were crying at the sight of my father's red face and my mother's weeping. When my brother stormed out of the room, telling my father to calm down, there was a fight and I saw my parents tugging at his arms very aggressively when he wanted to get back inside his room.

That was when I understood how much trouble I would get into if I ever had anything to do with a boy. I thought if my father ever found out I was kissing boys under the slide at the playground in kindergarten, his face would turn just as red.

"Only when you're married may you sleep with them." That's what my mother said when she tried to explain me why they were fighting. But I didn't understand why marriage was necessary for girls and boys to sleep next to each other. I thought if my mother had known how I was playing with boys in kindergarten, she would weep the same way.

When I turned six, I had just started the first grade and my mother had started working as a graphic designer and, at the same time, started a spa at our house. She needed more workers, more staff to give birth to this idea she had. She hired a couple of ladies and trained them to massage. She also hired an assistant who helped her with the graphic designs and another worker to keep the house safe from burglars or help around with the garden and fix stuff around the house.

My father was, and still is, a very busy man. He was always on his computer in his office, typing away. That's mostly what I remember about him in my childhood. He would take us to school and watch Popeye with us but mostly he would stare at his screen and type. I never felt close to my father; he barely played with us. I went with him to church sometimes, that's how we bonded. Although he was always home and I always saw him, and sometimes he would teach me how to read, I was not close to him at all. Looking back now, he was mostly elsewhere in his head.

I played often on my own, with my bike, the water hose or the neighbour's dogs. We had a big house. In Cambodia, people have gates in front of the house and walls around the house with barbed wires on the top. Our house had two floors with two staircases; one was spiral, made of wood, and the other was the "backdoor" one. We had five bedrooms, an office, two living rooms and a massive balcony. Some maids lived with us – they had a room fairly big near the kitchen at the back, and the new worker lived with us too but he slept outside next to our garage on a hammock. (I can't remember if he had an extra room.) Sometimes I would play with my maids and teach them English; sometimes I would play with my brother but he was not around so often. Mostly, I would play with my sisters, or alone.

On the day it all happened, I was playing in the front yard. I cannot remember where my sisters were but my mother was upstairs working on her project with our neighbour and the new assistant. My father was most likely in the office. My brother was out with friends. I was not allowed to play completely alone so the new worker, Bunni (pronounced *pu-ni*), was told to keep an eye out on me. He would lie in his hammock and sing along to Cambodian folk music on the radio that he would hold next to his head. Every now and then, he would look up to see if I was okay.

I don't remember how I started playing with him, but we played near his hammock, left of the garage, between the house and the walls protecting the house. We played with a hand mirror that I wanted to snatch away from him. He would make it harder and harder each time and whenever I won, he would hold me down on his lap and tickle me. Then he placed the mirror on a shelf above his head. I climbed up on his lap to reach for it, my feet on his knees. When I held the mirror in my hand, his head was under my dress. I felt like a pregnant lady. I felt him pull down my underwear and felt his tongue on my vagina.

I didn't know what to think of it; I just stared at this big round head under my dress moving and making kissing noises. *He's kissing me,* I thought. I didn't freak out at all. Instead, I placed my hand on his head as if it were my baby. I knew I was going to get in big trouble if my dad saw us, so I looked around and was glad that I didn't see anybody. He kept going and I stood still, watching the movements of his head. I thought it was weirdly pleasant. It felt strange but I liked it.

Then he took me in his arms, cupped my head in his hands and kissed me on the lips. His lips were so fat. It was harder to kiss him than the boys in kindergarten because his lips practically swallowed mine. He kissed me very passionately and I smelled his saliva breath all over my face. He stuck his tongue in my mouth, then I tried to imitate him like they did in the movies, and my tongue touched his teeth. I remember he had very bad crooked teeth and they were yellow too. I suddenly snapped out of it and thought it was the grossest thing ever. *He kissed me where I peed and now our tongues have touched,* I thought. I got up and ran into the house, up the back stairs and into my room where I changed my dress into jeans and a shirt; that way it would make it harder for him to pull down my underwear.

I thought about telling my mother, but I was afraid that she would cry and get really upset. I thought about telling her half the truth but something changed my mind and I cannot remember what it was. Soon enough, I forgot about it, but every now and then, I would remember and ask myself if I should tell anybody but I thought no one would believe me anyway because I was known to be a liar. That would have been a very awkward lie to tell.

We moved to a new house when I was seven. My mother needed more rooms and more staff. She was becoming well known in Phnom Penh. The ground floor was for my mother's spa and the first floor was the dining room and our bedrooms. The last floor was the roof with a jacuzzi and tiny gardens on the corners of the rooftop. There was also a bathroom with a shower. I loved to go swimming and had always dreamt of having a swimming pool in our house but we could never afford one. Instead, I felt lucky enough to have a jacuzzi; it was not as great as a pool but it was way more fun to bathe in there instead of the bathtub. There was a time, when it was the weekends, I would swim there seven times a day. My dad did not allow me to sit in the sun for too long and made me go downstairs to cool off but I always snuck back out when he went back to his laptop.

Bunni was watering the plants when I was bathing in the jacuzzi naked. My parents worried about me playing up there on my own because sometimes I would climb over the railing to the roof below where there were no railings. Bunni was supposed to keep an eye out for me. I knew it was a bad idea to swim naked and I knew my mother would have made me feel ashamed me for doing that. Especially when I saw him looking at me the way he was. He smiled at me, looked at me getting out of the water and quickly turned away, smiling to himself. I knew what he was thinking – I've seen that behaviour on HBO so many times before. It felt so playful, whenever I went under the water, he would do his chores and as soon as I came out, he would stare at me and get clumsy. Somehow I was able to control him and I found that amusing.

Suddenly, he dropped the hose and turned it off really quickly, then speed-walked towards me, taking massive steps. He grabbed me under my armpits and pulled me out of the jacuzzi, took me in his arms, like carrying a naked princess, and walked very fast to the bathroom. He was very hasty.

He placed me on top of the toilet with the lid shut and locked the door, then licked me out again. His head was the size of my waist, I noticed. I watched him do it, it was weirder seeing that and on top of it, it was not nice. His teeth rubbed against me and he was hurting me. Not extremely, but it did feel very uncomfortable. I tried to focus on something else, like the shells stuck on the wall or the mirror. Again, he took me in his arms and kissed me, smearing his big lips all over my face. I could not breathe. My body was clasped so tightly against his, I struggled to get out. I cannot remember how I managed to get away but somehow I unlocked the door and I ran downstairs. I stayed in my room until sunset.

Then my mother was finished with work and everybody was getting ready for dinner. I saw him at the front door doing some chores. I was angry at him, because this time it was not romantic at all. He left me feeling like I was food and I hated him for it. I didn't know why. I wanted him to get in trouble but I was scared to get in trouble myself. Mother walked out the front door and I snitched on him. "Bunni kissed me," I said, "on my lips."

"Bunni, you're not allowed to kiss my daughter, don't do that," she said politely in Khmer. He apologised, nodding his head to every sentence she said, folding his hands together asking for forgiveness with that typical forced apologetic smile. That made me angrier. He wasn't sorry for shit. He just wanted the awkwardness to be over. My mother told me off a bit for kissing him back so I didn't dare say more.

I cannot remember how many days or months later when my mother's assistant started touching me. It was also on the rooftop where I was sitting on his lap at a circular dining table under an umbrella patio, his fingers slipped in my underwear, which was all I was wearing. He asked me if I liked it and I said yes. It was only nice until I thought of his wife and baby who were just downstairs. His wife worked for my mother too, she was the receptionist at the spa. His baby couldn't walk yet and sometimes I would take care of him while they worked.

The door leading downstairs was slightly open. Anybody could have walked in on us any minute but he was so calm, as if he knew nothing was going to happen. I replayed a scenario in my head of the sound of his wife's footsteps going up the stairs and finding him doing this to me. I pictured her breaking down in tears and anger, throwing things at us because he was cheating on her with me. After all, it was a kind of romantic atmosphere, where he stared into my eyes the way the movie stars did in romance movies and continuously fiddling me down there.

I knew that you were not supposed to be romantic with no other but your wife or husband. I thought she would have gotten jealous or something like that. Oddly enough, I couldn't walk away from him and always came back and allowed him to do that to me. I don't know why. Looking back now, I assume it was because I knew how little gestures that I make, as simple as a smile or a deep stare into his eyes, affected his behaviour. He reacted the way I expected him to react, and whenever I pulled back or showed any signs of rejection, or signs that I might tell, his face would suddenly be covered with fear. For some reason, I liked to toy with that. It gave me a sense of power over his feelings. He would warn me not to tell anybody, but I would just give him an evil cheeky smile, said nothing back and skipped away. His face would turn worried and I would laugh at him.

I didn't tell anybody. His wife, Polly, was a nice woman and I didn't want to see her get upset with me. Every now and then, I would threaten him, sometimes for no particular reason. I just wanted to see him get worried for my own amusement or sometimes to get him to give me things, candy, or pens or whatever.

I became a manipulative and aggressive child, especially towards my sisters. The youngest one was the easiest to pick on. I would pinch and hit them, make them do things for me, blame things on them, lie about them to my parents. I lied about everything – even things that I didn't have to lie about, I did anyway. I made up stories and started stealing.

Overall, I was a polite child. We all were. We respected our parents, we listened, we finished our food, we didn't complain excessively, we didn't throw tantrums or create massive dramas. Yet compared to my sisters, I was the most difficult.

One day, when I was 10, I had a massive fit about nothing. We had moved again to a different house, my mother had rented two houses – one for her spa and one for us to live in. I was watching Bunni work in our garden. I started throwing shoes at him. He yelled at me and told me to stop but I just threw more at him. One hit his face and he got really mad and walked up to me and threatened to hit me, but I knew he wouldn't do it. I took a piece of cable from the ground and whipped him. He flipped out, asked me what was wrong with me, grabbed the cable out of my hands and dropped it in the bin. I ran and grabbed the hose behind him, and whipped him again and again. He tried to defend himself but I saw how the hose made red marks on his arms. The cook ran out and grabbed the hose out of my hands. She popped her eyes wide open in disbelief and shouted at me, telling me she was going to inform my mother.

Later on that day, Bunni was working at the spa, and the

cook and I went there to pick up my sisters. We waited for them in the car and Bunni saw us. He walked out and leaned in the driver's window and had a conversation with the cook. She translated for him and asked me, "Why did you do those things to him?"

"He knows exactly why," I replied, looking at my hands.

"He doesn't know why."

I actually didn't really know why either. I just felt angry. I just wanted to see him get hurt. I couldn't say that and I didn't really know why he deserved a whipping. I could not think of anything to say so I thought of a reason. "He did things to me when I was seven," I said.

There was a pause. He looked away and said, "Yeah, but that was a long time ago."

I wanted him to die.

The same evening, my parents heard the story and were furious. "You could have hit his eye and gotten him to hospital, Lucie!" They expected me to apologise or somehow give a really good reason for why I did that. "Do you think we have enough money to get him treatment?! What were you thinking?! He hasn't even done anything bad to you. He cares about you and your sisters!"

I ran upstairs to my room and cried. I wrote a letter to them: "I hurt him because he kissed me and licked my vagina when I was six and seven." I slipped it under their door and walked outside.

I sat alone, listening to the crickets and watching the geckos mesmerised by the light. My mother walked out the door and I saw the letter in her hands. She said nothing and just looked at me. I didn't want to look back at her. She sat on the other end of the bench and waited for me to say something but I wouldn't. My throat was clumped up; it felt like I had swallowed a sock but the tears wouldn't come.

"Is this true, did he do this to you?" she asked. I said nothing. She said nothing more. I didn't even care if I got in trouble for kissing him before getting married to him. I couldn't get married to someone who was 20 years older than me. She stared at the letter and stared into space. Both of us were waiting for the other to speak. I thought the situation was ridiculous so I walked back inside and locked myself in my room.

Nothing changed. He still worked for my family; we never spoke of it again. It couldn't have been big a deal, I thought.

We moved to Berlin when I was 11. My dad had cancer and we went to Europe to get him better treatment because [medical treatment in] Bangkok was too expensive. Culture shock was everywhere, but it was not hard for us to adapt. It was hard for my mom to adapt. All of a sudden everything is so liberal. Sex education is being taught in school openly? They talk about condoms in class? How to use them? She got so mad when she found out. This was when my dad was going through radiotherapy in England and she was fending for three kids in a foreign country without a job. As a 12-year-old, I was the only one she could talk to about the situation and how she really needed everyone to pray.

My dad was not around that much anymore because of the number of operations he had in England. He was not around to take me to church, which made me closer to my mother's faith. Soon, I converted because a guy in my class whom I was in love with was a Muslim and I wanted to feel desired by him. I thought that by converting, he would be impressed. I also thought it was nice to see my mother happy and proud of me for the first time.

I prayed with her, I went to the mosque with her and even attended Islamic lessons where we learnt how to recite the prayers and how to read and write in Arabic. We learnt all the rules, like how we should not eat with our left hand, how we should wash ourselves before praying, how girls should behave, how we were not allowed to have sex before marriage. She told me so many stories of women who have been left by their partners, or how young girls got pregnant when they were not physically ready to have a child and so on and so forth.

She made me promise that I will never have sex before marriage and that when I'm older I cannot do whatever I wanted with my body using the excuse, "It's my body, my rights." She explained that we were all here temporarily. We are only borrowing our bodies. When we die, we don't take anything with us, not our phones or clothes or even our bodies. Just our souls. And we will have to stand in front of the gates of Heaven and explain ourselves to Allah when He asks us what we have done.

"You take nothing but the good and bad you have done while you lived. Listen to your mother, for heaven lies beneath your mother's feet."

I broke my promise when I was 14 with my first boyfriend. He was a German boy. My dad read my Facebook messages and saw the whole detailed conversation I had with my best friend. He was furious and called my best friend's mother and told her about what he had just read. I came home from school, and from my father's tone of voice, I knew I was in deep trouble. He put a restraining order on my boyfriend. I was not allowed to have any sort of contact with him anymore. It broke my heart so much. He felt embarrassed in front of his parents. They knew he was sexually active and thought it normal at that age. Sure, I was a little young but if I was using protection and if no one was hurt, they didn't think it was a massive problem.

But my parents thought otherwise. It was exactly like when my brother was caught. I was so furious, I started blaming them for irrelevant things in my past to justify my behaviour. It escalated and when I ran out of excuses and arguments, the story of the molesters slipped out and suddenly, my dad stopped talking and looked at me concerned, as if he had no idea what I was talking about.

"What about that letter?" I asked.

"What letter?"

I looked at my mom and all she did was to sit silently beside him, looking at her nails nervously.

"I wrote you a letter when I was ten, Dad. And apparently nobody believed me."

My mother kept quiet. He was utterly shocked and said he had never seen a letter. I assumed my mother didn't tell him about it. I didn't know, and still don't know, why she didn't share that information with him. My father sat dumbfounded, said he was sorry that happened to me but he didn't ask *what* happened to me or *how* many times or anything because I was in the middle of being punished for having sex. Somehow, that fact slid under the carpet and we went back to arguing about the boyfriend.

I cried so loud that night. Mostly because I was not allowed to see my boyfriend anymore. However, when I had calmed down and stayed awake at night replaying the conversation, I couldn't understand that my parents cared more about me losing my virginity than someone taking advantage of me. I've only ever told one adult before, my best friend's mother, and she wept for me. I didn't understand why she wept for me. It's not like they hurt me or anything. Then she explained to me that things like that are not okay and I needed therapy. I asked myself why my parents didn't react the same way and assumed that maybe she was just an emotional woman.

Shortly before I turned 16, I became pregnant.

I had promised my mother, crying, that I would wait until I turned 18 to make love to my ex-boyfriend again. Because I thought I loved him that much. She believed me and was touched by my commitment. But then I met this boy in my class, who was bad, who was actually a knob head. He had issues, which required psychotherapy, but I was attracted to that. He gave me that rebellious excitement I never really had before: we smoked weed together, we skipped class together, we made fun of the world together. We also ignored the condoms and I got pregnant.

I didn't get on the pill because I thought I needed my parents' consent to get it and I didn't want my mother to know that I was still sexually active. She knew I had a new boyfriend but thought we were not having sex. I guess she suspected it the whole time because she always wanted me to stay at home. I snuck out of the house at night and met up with him, or he would sneak into my room and pretended like he came to visit me in the morning. We were really in love. And ignorant.

Our parents found out and there was a big drama. One of them told me I should go with my father to therapy, and discuss this matter and make a decision. When I told the therapist about my life and my childhood, I started crying more than ever. I have never cried about it before, I thought it was because of the hormones. The therapist advised me to get some help because what I had experienced was something traumatic. I didn't see it at all as traumatic. I didn't think of it that way. I didn't really think it was a big deal. I actually just wanted to make a point, to excuse myself for my aggressive behaviour, to give an explanation as to why I behaved inappropriately.

I didn't take the therapist's advice until after my daughter was born and I started going to school again. I didn't apply for therapy because of what had happened to me, but because I needed help getting organised, because I slacked off all the time. I was daydreaming; it was hard for me to keep track of everything and I thought I needed therapy to become a sane mother.

I went to see the same therapist and told him everything. He tried to help. He explained a lot of things about myself that I didn't understand but unfortunately, he acted too much like a father figure for me and, on top of it, didn't understand how a third world country functioned. You couldn't just sue a paedophile for something he did years ago in Cambodia. How were you even supposed to find him? Human trafficking, I heard, was practically run by the police and I was told they collected their taxes from brothels, so if I went to the police over there and filed a complaint saying that a man touched me 10 years ago, they would tell me to fuck off. They had better things to deal with.

I mean, in Phnom Penh, there were little girls aged 12 or so with red lipstick, sitting in front of a wooden, unstable muddy brothel with no expressions on their faces and people would drive by thinking that that was normal. I remember going to a friend's house once and on the way we counted the number of lipsticked women and girls. It was like a game: whoever counted the most, won. My friend's father asked me if I knew what those girls were. "They're prostitutes," I said casually. He swallowed and I could tell from his facial expression in the rear view mirror that he found it creepy I was making a game out of it.

My shrink could not understand the system there and forced my parents to do something about it – find the guy or make him confess. My dad had a huge argument with him, saying that he couldn't do anything because Bunni had gone back to the province, God knows where. But the other man, he still worked for my mother. Even after I told them about him too, they didn't fire him, they didn't question him. Not until the shrink told them to. And when they did, my mother told me to drop the topic: "He's apologised now." She said she told his wife about it, and saw her crying, telling her that if that were her child, she would react the same way or something like that.

There was once a Skype conversation and I heard his voice. I felt no emotion when he said he was sorry through Skype. I just wanted this whole thing to be over with because nothing would have changed if we sued him or pressed charges against him. His apology meant nothing to me. He didn't matter to me anymore. Seeing him get hurt would not have erased what happened to me.

What hurt me was the look on my mother's face when she didn't react. My father reacted once: he wept on my shoulders begging for forgiveness when he asked me what really went down. I didn't understand why she didn't – why didn't she freak out? Other adults who have heard the story went completely emotional and pitied me, but not my mother. She didn't even ask how it happened. She just kept looking at her nails.

She cried as if someone had died when she saw a picture of me and my first boyfriend kiss on the lips. She was on the bathroom floor and said she couldn't feel her legs anymore and wept so loudly, I was sure the neighbours heard her. But she didn't feel anything when she heard that someone who worked for her went behind her back and licked me out? Somehow that had no effect? And after she knew about the other man who fiddled with me, she didn't even fire him? She didn't want to believe me? Why would I lie about something like this? Did she really think I was that shallow? That I would go through all this drama to make a point? I got so mad. How could she possibly go ballistic about a kiss and then act like all of this doesn't even matter?

I knew she loved me but I felt she was ashamed of me somehow. Even though we all know that I shouldn't be ashamed and it wasn't my fault. Consciously, she knew it all too but she never hugged me or showed any kind of empathy.

I thought it was because she had too much pride or

something. Or that she didn't want to show that she pitied me because she didn't want me to be weak. She was not the type of woman that would tell her children how proud she was of them because she thought that would make us arrogant. Whenever I showed her my artwork, she would be brutally truthful about them, so I would push myself to be better. I thought she wanted me to toughen up. She didn't want me to use that excuse to whine and blame everything on my childhood or my parents. She wanted me to move on and accept that horrible things happen but you cannot let them pull you down – that no matter what, you have to go on.

It made sense to me, that you could not change what has happened in the past and you have to learn to live with that pain. I thought that was the reason why she didn't react. She didn't want me to be a pussy.

It was much later that I figured out she had been abused herself. I knew her friend raped her before she met my dad. The man thought she was not a virgin anymore because she had had an American boyfriend before. But she was. She told me how much it hurt her and how she didn't tell anybody in her family for about thirty years.

She also told me once that someone tried to rape her when she was a child. She was almost suffocated at night and someone tried to get in her pants but failed. She had many brothers and her cousin was there for a visit; she didn't know who it could have been. Ever since then, she was always scared to sleep in the dark.

One time we sat at the dinner table – this was a time when the whole family were fed up with me – everyone had something negative to say about me, how I was not contributing enough, how I went out too much, how I was neglecting my daughter, how I was selfish. My siblings teamed up and threw a bunch of hateful things at me: "You never do this and you're always like that, you don't care for anyone but yourself." My parents sat beside each other agreeing to what they were saying and adding some more, "You need to be more like this, get on top of your shit, stop whining and blaming everything on us. You're an adult now, you're responsible for your own actions."

I felt so much pressure, defending myself against four other people, almost every single time we had dinner. I just blurted out my traumatic events as a defence mechanism, as an explanation of why I am the way I am and they should be more empathetic towards me.

My mother flipped out and told me something I have never heard of before. "Do I go around and treat people horribly and selfishly because other people have done horrible things to me? No. You know, when I was four or five," she started crying and hesitating, "My mother never paid attention to me. We were eight children, can you believe that? *Eight.* We were poor and my parents were always busy, selling things, my mother sold food. You know this, Lucie. You know, even our floor was still dirt because we could not afford a real floor. We had to build our roof ourselves. We were living off scraps. I had to take care of myself because everybody was struggling to survive. We had nothing and you're sitting here and complaining that we did not give you enough, how do you think that makes me feel? I always played on my own, no one watched over me. I was the youngest one, sometimes my brothers would watch me but not always. I did not have anything you have now. I had to earn it all myself; did I use any excuses for why I could not do it? No. Lucie, life must go on no matter what. You cannot just blame everything on other people. I could also do that, you know, I could also start drinking and say it was because of the rape. But did I do that? No. I have to take responsibility for my own life. Even if… one time…" she had difficulty breathing and articulating her words, "when I was four or five, I think… I was playing alone and then these men came up to me and cornered me. I was so scared…" She wept. My dad stared into space beside her.

"You cannot imagine what they did to me, these group of men… I couldn't scream, I couldn't…" she cried and couldn't finish her story.

"I'm sorry that happened," my dad muttered. "No child should ever have to go through that."

She couldn't breathe. I couldn't watch her tell the story anymore. I barged into my room holding my head, trying to get the picture of my four-year-old frightened mother with these strange men out of my head. What they might have done to her, how they must have hurt her.

I felt so stupid for complaining about what happened to me since that was nothing compared to what she had had to experience. I thought about how much she has achieved in her life and how she didn't let that horrible story be an excuse for anything. I felt weak compared to her. I blamed a lot of things about myself on my parents. For never really being around when I was a child. And there was my mother, a woman who has been through much more horrid things and she was able to get out of the slums and fund her university studies, and marry a nice man and move to Europe. I felt small when I looked at her. I was spoiled from the beginning, failed in school, got pregnant, did drugs. And this woman who has endured so much pain still lives her life with a smile on her face while raising an ungrateful child.

I wanted to bang my head against the wall because I felt so ashamed of myself and what kind of person I have become. It became so clear to me, why she couldn't react. How could she have known how to react to her daughter's story if she didn't even have the chance to process her own trauma? I blamed her so often for not being there for me when that happened to me. I accused her of so many things, I insulted her, and I made her cry countless times.

I only had the picture of my four-year-old mother crying out for help. I wish I could have reversed her tears, I wish I could have saved her.

When I look at my daughter now and I have these thoughts, panic attacks arise. I get all emotional and worried, like a mad woman. I think that I'm trapped; I'm going to be worrying forever now. Things like this are way beyond your control. It could happen to anyone at any time.

Far away, or in the same house.

an email
27th January 2015

Dear Lin,

I try to write every day ever since I managed to buy my own laptop. In the past few years, I've realised I think about things differently than others, and it's hard for me to concentrate on the choice of words while I talk, so this is why I write. When I do this, I have a better understanding of my agitated thoughts. I've been writing diaries since the fourth grade. It helps me organise my thoughts so that when someone is arguing with me, I already have my arguments ready in my head.

I write a lot about my everyday life and sometimes about my dreams and goals, but mostly about mistakes that I'm too ashamed to admit to anyone. It's nice to have someone read stuff I write. I secretly always wanted people to open my diaries and read my mind so that I wouldn't be misjudged. I think that happens way too often. I feel like there's a reason for why people do the things they do; the reasons may not be legitimate or excusable, but it's still an explanation. People always look at what lies on the surface, at the obvious. They rarely try to see deeper, the cause of it all, how it all happened. You can always trace things back to the beginning and find the unseen pieces that affected people's actions.

I wish my parents took more time to analyse me as a child, so they could question why all of a sudden I had difficulties concentrating in school – daydreaming all the time, making trouble and, most importantly, why my libido was so high. Instead, they just assumed, "That's just the way she is." And went back to work. If they hadn't done that, maybe I would have been able to heal faster… I do not know. But I cannot blame them for it anymore, now that I understand who they are, how they see things. They just did not know any better.

I think there's always a reason why a child suddenly does "bad things": they do not just come out of nowhere. But parents try to discipline their children more often than trying to understand them. It's easier to blame everything on the obvious, I guess. However, this led me to lie constantly because I was afraid of the consequences. Lying became such an everyday thing, I lied out of habit, and as a result, no one ever believed me or relied on me anymore.

I thought that's probably why my mother didn't react at first because she thought I was lying to get the molester punished for my actions. But it's not that. I think I reminded her of something really traumatic that happened to her, and she went blank which caused her actions to be unusual. The easiest thing for her was to push it under the carpet and go on living life. Whenever the topic of my child molester came up, she behaved so calmly and normally as if there were no problems. I think it was just her repressing everything.

I'm glad that Clara (see Chapter 4) called me and told me about you. I've been waiting to share this story and what I had learnt from it for a long time. Hoping that one day it would reach out to a frightened little girl and give her some light. I'm very passionate about helping women who are stuck in fear and confusion. Giving them a home for shelter or a hideout is one thing, but trying to calm their souls is another.

LIFE NOW

I was Christian in Cambodia and I became Muslim when I moved to Berlin, then I was nothing. As soon as I was 13 or 14, I gave up on religion. I felt my parents were delusional. I think there are great morals, but even without religion, they would be there anyway.

I liked it when guys looked at me, like in the movies. I wanted to take control of the situation but that never happened. I wanted to be nice and I let them do whatever. I just didn't know when to say "no". I'd let them. It would be too embarrassing for me to say "no". I would be like, just get it over with. I would hate the situation. It would be a quick, unsatisfying thing.

I have this vision that I'll land up on the beach and have my own shop. Just to be self-sufficient, emotionally and financially. I want to do this thing. I want to create visuals and all that, pursue my talents and all that boring stuff. I want to be successful but not in terms of money. I want to be successful in terms of reaching out more to people. For them to be ready for what I have to say.

I don't think my story of child sexual abuse will define me if I speak about it, but it's about what I'll do with it. What I'll do next. I'm really passionate about fucked up people, because I feel it. You can tell they're scared. They have that vibe.

If you have the power to give a little light in the darkness, why worry about your own troubles, when you can share light with others? It's like that motherly thing that I have: if that were my kid, how would I deal with it?

11

NIKITA

21-year-old Nikita is half-American and half-German. She moved to Berlin from the US at the age of 16. She was molested by the sons of family friends when she was nine, and was later abused by a boyfriend. He kept her captive in his room for days on end, and sexually mistreated her throughout the relationship, including various accounts of physical abuse. Lucie (see Chapter 10) is her best friend.

....

Café Böse Buben Bar, Berlin
19th May 2015

> *"Wie man in den Wald hineinruft, so schallt es heraus."*
> (German saying: What goes around, comes around)

That's a great saying. I think it sums it up nicely. I'm not religious at all but I was very curious as a child. My parents were not religious and were very open. I read a lot on spirituality as I found it very fascinating. People can create something out of it. People do different things to navigate through life.

I have a very small but supportive family: just me, my mom and my dad. I'm an only child. My parents are pretty funky or alternative. We were poor when I was little. I spent my early childhood in a somewhat poor area. But then my dad had a corporate job and we moved somewhere nicer. I'm an artist. My parents have always been very supportive of that.

THE ABUSE

My parents have these friends, quite far away in California. Throughout my life, my parents have been friends with them. They were artists too, nice, rich people. They have two sons: one is younger than me, the other older than me.

Before the little one was born, I'd play with the older one. He was not my friend. I was just expected to play with him whenever our parents meet up. He seemed like he had social problems, like he was autistic, perhaps.

Once, we were playing doctor. I'm still not sure what happened, I knew it was his idea. It was just a kid thing. He would tell me about what this older girl would do with him. He'd say, "Let's do this thing that this girl and I would do together."

I'd say, "What?"

We played the game but I did not like it very much.

They have this very big house, and we'd visit maybe every two years. Once, he came to stay at my house, which was rare. He was in my room; we were playing.

He said, "Say, do you remember that game that we used to play?"

"No," I responded quickly. I remembered but I felt weird. I didn't want to play that. He was very mean to me for the rest of the day. He broke one of my toys.

At dinner, I had this weird, metallic taste in my mouth. I don't know whether it was psychosomatic – I just remember using it as a good excuse to get away from him and lie down.

Another time, when I was older, they had a pool. They were very rich. He was about 13 already. He was making comments about my body and how I was developing all the time. I was nine. He would act different in front of the grown-ups. I felt I didn't want to hang around him.

He tried to force me to go into their pool with him. He asked profusely in front of my parents, and my mom was like, "Oh, the boys are so friendly! Why don't you go into the pool with them?"

His little brother was there too, three years younger than me. He made this younger brother touch me. They were fondling and poking me. So I moved to the other side of the pool. I told them I was scared of going under water because when I was little, I fell into a fountain, and one time my dad tried to teach me how to swim by throwing me in a pool. So both brothers went to get me, and pulled me underwater where they continued to touch me.

Then it got late and everyone started getting ready for bed. My parents were staying in another wing of the house, it was so big. I had to share the eldest boy's bedroom; I had my own mattress. There was a huge bathroom which connected the two bedrooms of the boys. The older brother had a bunk bed. I felt uncomfortable. But his parents were really nice so I didn't want to make a scene.

The adults left. The older one said, "We should play that game that we used to play."

"Why?" I shot back. I was creeped out.

He said, "You should play with me."

When we were little kids, he had this old cereal box with coloured construction paper in it, cut into strips. He would say, "This is the tool: take my temperature." He would play pretend. For some reason, he still had this box even though he was considerably older.

He said, "We have to go to the bathroom." He took me and locked both doors.

It involved objects, including the handle of a hairbrush and I had to do things with them. I tried to get away but he stopped me and sat me on my legs. I didn't know what to do because it would be embarrassing to make a scene and I didn't want to scream because I was not sure I could be heard, the place was so big.

Every time, he would tell me about that older girl. She was 16 at the time. I met her actually – her name was Constantina. She had done something to him; I assume that an adult must have done something to her. These kids must have learnt this behaviour somewhere.

Whoever started this was really bad, because this behaviour was aggressive and forceful.

GROWING UP

As I grew older, I started reading up on these things. I was trying to figure it out. It was pretty hardcore, I suppose, but it's a different story when an adult is doing these things to you. It's obviously wrong in those situations. My situation is a lot more confusing because of the ages of the people involved, us being minors.

I'm not sure if it was the same night, but he made me play this dumb spy game where we had to listen in on our parents' private conversations. He made up these rules that if we heard something that we were not supposed to hear, like bad language, whoever heard it would have to kiss the other. He would grab my face to make out. I hated it.

Before I moved away, I had a farewell party. He was there, staring at the corner, smirking at me. Everyone was like, "Who's this kid?" And I was like, "Yeah, that's my parents' friends' kid. He's weird."

I was a super shy kid. I was dressing up at the age of nine like a goth. Everyone thought I was depressed. I was just into it. My parents were supportive of my interests.

One time in school, I was sitting at the back and cutting my arm hair with scissors because I was so bored. A substitute teacher thought I was cutting myself so I had to go into therapy. Everyone also thought I was anorexic because I was skinny.

When I turned 13, I started internalising all the things that everyone assumed about me. I rejected my femininity after being dumped by my first boyfriend who completely used me for sex. I shaved my head completely and wore no make-up. My hobbies included skateboarding and boxing. I liked the adrenaline rush. I wanted people to think that I was super strong, which I guess I can be, but that's just one side of me. It was just too forced back then. Too over the top and unhealthy. I wanted the world to know that I could not be messed with anymore. I would get into street fights and that kind of crap.

My dad probably has some underlying anger management issues which he is good at masking usually. He has totally flipped out on me in the past, yelling and throwing me to the floor. My mom thinks that I got these anger tendencies from him.

I was into punk and I was more socially accepted as I grew older. I had a lot of friends. Here [in Germany], I don't have friends. I have my two sides – I can be a total loner and want to be alone, and I can be an adrenaline junkie.

BOYFRIENDS

My first boyfriend took my virginity. He convinced me to have sex with him. Right after, he told a friend to tell me that I had been dumped. And then he had sex with these other girls at his house directly afterwards. I felt very taken advantage of.

I felt that being a girl was the worst thing. You get fucked over. I looked at the other girls – they were trying to attract guys' attention. I was going to be different – a girl and a boy. Just a human.

I started cutting myself quite regularly. I still have some scars on my thighs. I never wanted anyone to see them because I didn't want anyone to think I wanted attention. I just did it because I liked the way it felt. I liked how extreme and raw it felt. I liked most things to feel extreme back then.

I moved to Berlin on my 16th birthday. From having a ton of friends, I had no one. My German was shaky. I didn't want to change my personality. I would continue doing what I used to do – going to punk shows and taking drugs and such. I would drink too much. Maybe my parents would say, "You shouldn't drink so much" but no more than that. I felt numb, and was trying to trick myself that I was having fun.

I was really lonely.

DRAWING THE LINE

I got kicked out of the German school. I hadn't gone to classes. I hated school and simply didn't even care that they wanted to kick me out.

So I got kicked out and I was really lonely and I met this guy called Wolf. We were like-minded: he was into metal and he likes to read a lot, so I was like, that's my type! But it got really weird half a year after I went out with him. He was schizophrenic. He has mental illness in his family.

I was really close to him. Subconsciously, he saw the vulnerability that I had and totally latched onto me. He started getting mean, with insults. Before, he'd be really nice. I thought I must have done something wrong. He would say, "Why are you such a bitch, why are you such a whore?"

It escalated. One day, he completely flipped out and held a knife to my neck and twisted my arm. He would beat me, pinch me or twist my arm. I had a hard time drawing the line. I kept breaking up with him and then he'd stalk me.

He'd tell me that I'm the crazy one or he'd say, "Stop playing the abuse victim. You need to get over it. You're just projecting what your other people did on me."

I found it so difficult: how could someone close to me say all that?

I made a list of the things that he's done to me for my therapist. He'd pressure me into doing sexual things that I didn't like, over and over again. We would be a natural couple, with romance and kissing, and then it'd become: "Why aren't you climaxing fast enough? You suck at this, you aren't sexy enough." After all the insults, I'd want to stop having sex. Then he'd say "You can't keep me hanging. You'd have to keep going. I'm a man."

He would physically force me to do stuff.

During one of the worst times, he smashed things, beat me, raped me, and kept me in his room for five days. I couldn't even go to the bathroom. He told me, "Look at what you did to me. You made me so angry. This is what you deserve."

He did what he wanted. I was fighting back at first but it never helped. I gave up after a while. I felt like a beaten dog, or an empty shell. Or a blown up sex-doll.

After a huge screaming fit, he said to me, "Now I get the pussy I deserve." He held me down and started to have sex with me. I tried to fight him off but he was so much stronger than me.

Then, suddenly, he started crying. I thought, OK, now what? I could not fathom that this same asshole was trying to rape me. He was crying and kissing me, and petting me and apologising. It didn't make any sense.

I told him about my childhood sexual abuse, and he used that against me. He'd say, "You're pathetic, you can't get over this stuff. You're so repressed." But at other times, he would

be really nice, and he'd say, "This must have hurt you so bad."
It varies. He would say, "You're tripping." And then another
time, "Oh, you poor thing."

I have not been with him for a long time. But when I see
him, my brain turns off. It's like he has a remote control over
me. He would stalk me. He would just turn up. He'd say, "I'll
come to your house now if I can't get what I want."

For a long time, I was too embarrassed to tell anyone
because I'm not that kind of person. Not the kind of woman
who lets people have their way with me. That's what I like
to think. I want to have my self-respect. I would come back
from seeing him and say, "I had a really fun time," when
people asked, when in actual fact, I had been held down,
insulted, and had cried for hours and hours.

School helped me; it was a distraction from all the
horrible things he would do to me daily. I would put my
heart into it. I'd help my mom cook. Again, I would put
my soul into it. Everything I did, I would do it 150 percent.
Everyone was like, "She's doing so good! She's into it, she
does her homework, she's helping around the house. And
she doesn't have as many friends as she used to, so she doesn't
party so hard."

I didn't have friends because Wolf would not let me.

THERAPY

I'm still at the beginning of my therapy.

It's really nice to go somewhere, to see the therapist,
because I can be totally honest. I didn't tell anybody anything
about what Wolf was doing to me for a long time. I was

afraid of being judged, making people worry about me, and half the time, most of the harsh advice people give me is already in my head, I'm already beating myself up about all of this.

I also don't want to be pitied. The situation with Wolf was a lot worse than I could handle. He had tactics: he'd get me to do things that he wanted me to do. He'd used the things that he knew about me as psychological leverage over me.

I had this fantasy of being a fantastic girlfriend in the beginning. But now I have revenge fantasies. I want to mess his life up – to spit in his drink and turn his friends against him, ruin his life. But I don't want to stoop to his level. I tried everything to get him to stop: the silent treatment, ignoring him, even shouting back, or being quiet and agreeing with him. Nothing worked.

Nothing he says, he means. And even if what he says is good, I can't take it seriously.

I thought, why do I go back to him so much? I don't know what to do. I'm at a total blank. I feel like I have lost control over my life. I'm really trying – I go to therapy multiple times a week.

I just want to move on. I feel this thread that still attaches me to him: I'd run into him. I block him from all my devices but he'd come up with a new email address and get in touch with me.

The worst thing was when I was somewhat abducted and kept in his room for days. I was naked because he would take and hide my clothes so I couldn't leave. I had peed on his bed, because I couldn't go to the bathroom. He wouldn't let me. I felt like a war prisoner. I said I needed to go to the bathroom but he wouldn't let me so I peed on his bed. He didn't say anything. He took all my clothes so I couldn't leave so I was constantly naked too.

When people hear this story, they would think that he's some weird, evil person all the time. But he's super intelligent. He's very good at reading people. He was so nice in the beginning. He got me to like things I don't always like, because he is so manipulative. Like he trained me. It's hard to process that. It's really weird.

When I broke up with him last summer, I had to clean up everything – put my life back together again. It took me some time to get a routine set up in my life.

I had this epiphany: I had been scared for my life. Every day, I felt like I could easily be murdered by him. It was really intense to admit that to myself.

I have to let go. I realise now that I have this leverage over him just as he did over me. Sometimes I just want revenge. People say that the best revenge is happiness, so I have to let go.

Wolf's mom should have stepped in. She didn't want to deal with the fact that her son was out of line, doing totally evil things. It made her feel better about herself maybe to see it happen to somebody else in a very twisted way. Either way, I felt like I was alone.

A school canteen, Berlin
20th May 2015

It all seems a bit cloudy to me. The pool thing, and the sleepover thing: whether it's the same day or not.

My ex-boyfriend, he knew that. He'd use this against me, "You're making stuff up." He'd say that maybe something worse happened and I couldn't remember it. He used that as leverage. That was super messed up.

That's the kind of thing I'm thinking about lately, putting pieces together.

IMPACT OF ABUSE

I haven't been talking to my therapist on the child sexual abuse very much, more on the recent boyfriend stuff. It helps me to sort things out in my head, you know. I lose track of what I'm doing. It's like what we talked about yesterday, I have anger like a wound-up toy car. Once there, I zip away pretty fast.

I find it hard to see movies with abuse in it. I really like slasher movies and stuff. There's a Japanese film, *Ichi the Killer* – it's full of rape and awful things. That was the point of it, to depict the evils of the world. I remember watching it and feeling strange for a couple of days afterwards.

I found my sexuality has been warped. The objectivity of women... If you're in this situation, like the situation I was in, you'll try to make the best out of it I guess, try to find something nice about it. They say that your first sexual experience will shape the rest of your sexual experiences. I feel that there's some truth to that, especially if you're young, as that will be true of any experiences when you're young: it'll affect your life.

Sexual abuse can take away something psychologically. It goes both ways: some people have a very strong libido. Some people can be traumatised and don't ever want to be touched and stuff.

I feel like caught between being passive and dominant sexually. For me, when I'm comfortable with someone, I'd fall into the more submissive end of the spectrum. It's not necessarily what I need for myself. If it's somebody I don't know very well, I'd go for a more dominating role.

If somebody's not attentive, or not interested, I'd just drop it. I'd feel super scared. I'd feel insecure. My relationships last a very long time. Which can be a good thing but not in the last case. There's a thin line that goes between loyalty and addiction.

With my last boyfriend, I was super comfortable. Wolf was patient. He's not like that anymore. That's how he lured me in. I was a hundred percent myself around him. It's that comfort of somebody who knows you so well, even if he's really mean to you. I was like, "You should understand that you're really hurting me as you know me better than anyone else."

I don't really have very high ambitions by other people's standards. I just want to be successful with my art. Just within my community. I don't need to have a lot of money. Just a handful of friends that I'm really close to. I want to be in a space that you'd feel comfortable in, with a lot of inspiration, and love and creativity.

12

ALICE

27-year-old Alice works for a charity based in Singapore. She was abused by her father when she was nine. The following year, he was reported by her school teacher to the police. He was sentenced to prison for twenty years and is due to be released in a year's time. Alice was put in a shelter immediately after the case was reported. Subsequently, she moved to another shelter after the home closed down and then spent time with a foster family. She moved back into her family home when she was 17. She now lives with her mother, and is currently single.

....

Burger King, Singapore
24th December 2015

It changed my life, though I am not quite sure if it's for better or for worse. Having been through this, fate moulded me somewhat differently. I turned out slightly bitter but nonetheless, rather thankful. Why? Because life is not always picture-perfect. But it could have been worse. Still, it feels complicated because there's some kind of damage that you cannot undo forever.

Till now, I am not sure what to expect when he comes back. I cannot embrace him fully. For most of my life, he was absent, and when he was around, he was a figure I feared.

FORGIVENESS AND ACCEPTANCE

I feel sad that forgiveness and acceptance is not a given after 20 years. No doubt he has served his sentence, and he has paid the price for it. But there is an unspeakable void. When he comes out of prison, it will never be like how it used to be. Maybe it will bring forth another set of challenges, so there is a lot of fear and uncertainty. I do hope he comes out alive, so that at least there's a chance for a family reunion.

My emotions feel tangled. Is it that I've accepted what happened, but I've not forgiven? Have I healed? I wish I can find closure but there's never a time when I could talk about this without crying. I'm really looking forward to the day when I can do so gracefully, without being stirred so much.

I do not know what it takes to achieve this tranquillity. I wished I knew how, then I could work towards it. Each time I talk about it, I am reminded of the guilt that I bear and the shame I had caused to my family. It is not just about what my father did, it is the consequence and aftermath of a broken family. This is not just about me; it is also about him being a father to my sisters, a husband to my mother, a son to my grandmother and a brother to my uncles and aunties. All of these changed overnight. Fault aside, I feel I caused this missing piece in their lives.

He did it but I was part of the game. If it had not been reported, maybe it would have been different. Having reported him, I was guaranteed some years of safety. But it was never my intention to jail him.

REPORTING THE ABUSE

I only wanted to stop him. It was my teacher who reported him, without first letting me know what she would do. She merely followed the standard operating procedures then. I did not know it would be this disastrous. I put up with it for two years before sharing it with my teacher.

When it first started, I told myself that maybe it was a once-off. But it only grew more frequent. Nobody knew about it. I would usually be alone in the room. A few times, he reminded me not to report it to the police. I could have reported him but I couldn't and I didn't want to. I went to a trusted source, my teacher, trusting that she would be objective and tell me first what she would do; perhaps she could speak to my family.

She didn't do any of that. There was no damage control after it was reported to the authorities either. Immediately, I got plucked out of my family.

The relationship with my family deteriorated. It took many years to restore. The impact on my mother was too much – she developed high blood pressure and depression, which affected my sisters too. There, I was, in the shelter, away from the brunt of the trauma. My sisters had to overcome my mother's tantrums. Worse yet, all of them had to face questions and gossip from everyone else.

I told you about the letter that my sister wrote me. I believe it was not written out of blame but more like out of desperation. My sister's only five years older than me. What else could she have done?

MY MOTHER

My mum does not seem to trust me enough. I'm the youngest kid. I do not know whether it's because of this.

Communicating with my mother is a challenge. Whatever I say, she'll tend to seek a second opinion or some sort of validation from other sources. It does not help now that I am older, with my own set of views and values. Sometimes, I would rather she not ask me anything in the first place! In her eyes, I am immature and inexperienced. But now, I am an adult and I ought to be taken seriously.

I feel sorry for my mom, but the way we relate to each other is still very warped. The love that we have for each other is very rough and tough. Most times, we disagree and my sisters will try to mediate. That's not how we should exist. I am not sure whether the brokenness led to this, but it would be fair to say it contributed.

I did not spend much of my childhood with my mom. It was just here and there. She was not with me all the way. Given the way things are, it's hard to establish empathy or some sort of understanding.

FAMILY

I live with regret because there are many things I cannot compensate for. I cannot compensate for his absence; I cannot compensate for the lost time. I cannot compensate for the kind of pain that my family had to go through.

If he comes out of prison, will he feel the distance? It's a pity if it turns out to be a poor reconciliation, especially if this is something that he has been looking forward to having in old age. But I know my mother will never forsake him.

He still gets along with my sisters. They write letters regularly. I only replied to his letters once. We never discuss the issue of his return publicly. It's like scratching the wound, you know? I'd rather keep it under wraps until the time comes.

I hope to show more tender loving care to my mum. I hope she'll disagree with me less often. Even though I may have the intention, my actions are still not aligned. I only have them in my heart.

When my father comes out of prison, we'll let bygones be bygones. Can we live together? I'd think twice!

THE ABUSE

As a child, I used to do physiotherapy. The therapist used to say: practise the exercises at home. One day, my father said he'd do the therapy with me. It was unusual because my mother used to do it all the time and he never offered to help at all.

He put the pillow cover over my eyes. The next thing I knew, he had taken off my pants. But there was no penetration or anything like that but a touch here, a touch there. That was one time.

I was nine. The frequency was once every two weeks. We would watch TV. He would ask me to touch whatever. At first, you'd tell yourself, maybe it would be just this once or twice. Maybe it happened accidentally, but the frequency became worse. My mother suspected something but did not ask him directly. When she did ask him, he assured her that there was nothing happening.

More and more, he was getting worse, more intense. He told me once or twice, "You cannot report me to the police." I listened to what he said. I did not tell and I did not want to tell either. One day, I went to a classmate's house. I shared it with her privately and we kept it to ourselves.

DISCLOSURE AND THE AFTERMATH

One day, I confided in my teacher after school had ended. The following day, an officer came to look for me in class and I did not go home after that. It all happened so quickly, like Speedy Gonzales! I did not know when I left home for school that morning, that I was not going back. There was no chance for any parting words.

I did not have contact with my family for the entire year, except the one time when I used a pay phone to call home. I spoke to my mom and she sounded fine, happy even, to hear from me. But it was a 10-cent-coin pay phone. What could we have said in so short a conversation? It was just a matter of seconds. When it came to the face-to-face meeting some time later, my mother said, "See! What have you done!"

On the day that my father was sentenced, my mother came to school. She was very affected by it, so she sat in my classroom and cried.

When I first entered the shelter, I missed my family home.

I missed my mother, like any child. I did not know that my mum was angry at me for what had happened.

COUNSELLING

I had a psychologist and a psychiatrist then, and every time I met them, I had to repeat the story. They would say to me, "I heard that your mother *blah, blah, blah*. How do you feel?" After a while, I felt as though I was repeating the same things, and getting upset over and over again. I figured it was easier to keep quiet.

Over time, I realised that no matter what I shared with these professionals, there was nothing that they could do to help me. They could not stop my mother. I tell them everything yet everything remains the same. My mother's still angry and I'm still sad.

After the sentencing was done, the authorities had to see me for a while. Then the frequency changed. During the investigation period, it was every week, then it became once every two weeks, then once a month. Then I was referred to a new psychologist. I changed to a different one who remained all the way until I moved to foster care. And then the psychologist said, "You're OK now."

When I was in secondary one or secondary two, I stayed in a shelter. There was a psychologist whom I saw once a month. And then it became once every few months. While in foster care, I would meet them when I needed a listening ear to share my woes.

At 17, I returned to my family home. The authorities allowed this gradually. I went home a few days a week when my mother was not working. After half a year of this, I could actually go home. So when I started going to a polytechnic, I was home entirely.

MY MOTHER AND I

I do not like to talk about this, because I get overwhelmed by emotions. But I hope that this may help somebody somewhere, somehow.

My mother has had many challenges in life. She overcame them with her own will and grit but that has also made her bitter about life. She's not well-educated, so she gets respite by nagging and blaming others. She'd say something to spite you even though she may not mean it. My uncle says that my mother is a tough nut because she lacks love. Life has not been good to her. She does not know what tender loving care is.

WHAT YOU BECOME

It's not about what happens to you, it's about what you become.

I remember bumping into a friend many years later after we had left the home. She said she had been on drugs and was doing rehabilitation at a shelter. Other friends were starting to build their families and seemed happy.

At every crossroad, you have a choice. If I had a choice, I'd rather choose to do nothing but I feel that I owe it to my mother to do well. The only way I can help her is to take care of myself. I've got to make sure I do that.

The only thing I ask of her is that she lets me do whatever I want to do. She's a big part of my motivation. Sometimes, I find her a "thorn" because she's the only person who can make me so angry and so upset. No one else can stir me up like she can! But I also realised she can have a huge impact because she means a lot to me.

To put it more crassly, if a lot of shit happens to you, don't become shitty! Get out of that shit and turn into something good. The more you go to the dark side, the harder it is to turn back. One thing leads to another and every action comes with consequences. You must decide to do the right thing by making a conscious and deliberate choice.

Life will put you in shit. Life is full of shit. You're still accountable to yourself, whether or not you choose to get out of it.

Be thankful – that's your silver lining. Be thankful that you're alive because your presence can mean a lot to someone. Be thankful for the people who stand by you.

Be thankful that you have gotten this far.

It is not by chance. It is by choice.

PART II:
THE PROBLEM OF
CHILD ABUSE

THE PROBLEM OF CHILD ABUSE
by Dr. Daniel Fung

Child abuse is a complex concept involving both social and cultural issues, its definitions determined by the social mores of the day. Children had little rights in the past and more than 100 years ago, children were considered property of their parents, much like animals were the property of their owners. In fact, the Royal Society for the Prevention of Cruelty to Animals in the United Kingdom was formed some eight years before the Royal Society for the Prevention of Cruelty to Children. These societal attitudes towards children and their development changed as knowledge about parenting and child protection became widely disseminated.

Because of these varying definitions, it is not surprising that societies across the world have very different estimates of children who have been abused. Child abuse continues to be a contentious issue across societies. For example, young girls in parts of Africa, Middle East and Asia are circumcised for religious reasons, but such an act would have qualified for child abuse in other parts of the world. The World Health Organization (WHO) estimates that almost 200 million women have had this procedure done on them even though there are many potential health risks (WHO 2017).

DEFINITIONS OF CHILD ABUSE

Definitions of child abuse have ranged from overly inclusive ones, such as causing harm to the development of a child, to narrowly defined ones found in the laws of the land. Generally, child abuse is an exploitation of children with disregard towards their health and development. A child would be considered abused if he or she is persistently treated in an unacceptable way for a given culture and time. An isolated incident where there is a lapse in the usual protection of a child should not be considered a case of abuse.

For the sake of convenience and classification, child abuse is sometimes divided into four main categories:

- Physical abuse – the inflicting of physical injuries through the use of excessive force
- Psychological or emotional abuse – the use of coercive, demeaning and detached behaviour that affects the emotional and social development of a child
- Neglect – the failure to provide basic shelter, supervision, care and support for proper development of a child
- Sexual abuse – the use of children for adult sexual gratification

Many studies have shown that abuse does not necessarily follow these well-defined categories, but it often occurs together. In Singapore, the official figures for child abuse are small compared to many parts of the world.

Sexual abuse is a term which most people think they know, but when asked for a definition they often come up with differing views. A broad-based definition can be one that is adopted by the WHO, along with the International Society for Prevention of Child Abuse and Neglect (ISPCAN) (WHO and ISPCAN 2006), which states:

"Child sexual abuse is the involvement of a child in sexual activity that he or she does not fully comprehend, is unable to give informed consent to, or for which the child is not developmentally prepared and cannot give consent, or that violates the laws or social taboos of society. Child sexual abuse is evidenced by this activity between a child and an adult or another child who by age or development is in a relationship of responsibility, trust or power, the activity being intended to gratify or satisfy the needs of the other person".

In Singapore, the Ministry of Family and Social Development (MSF 2016) defines sexual abuse as:

"When a person in a position of differential power causes a child to be exposed to, to be used as passive stimuli for, or to be directly involved in the performance of sexual acts for their own sexual stimulation or gratification. This includes having the child view pornography, be exposed to sexually explicit conversation, to be the recipient of sexual acts, and to perform sexual acts on another person."

Put simply, sexual abuse is any form of non-consensual sexual contact. This can happen to any gender and at any age. On one end of this spectrum is rape while on the other is exposing children to inappropriate sexualised materials.

A GLOBAL PICTURE OF SEXUAL ABUSE

ISPCAN has been conducting a worldwide survey every two years since 1982. In their most recent iteration (Dubowitz et al 2016), 73 countries were surveyed and most countries had clear definitions of child sexual abuse although this was less true of Asian countries. With regard to social conditions, it is interesting that although 85% of respondents in Asia and Africa consider child marriage as sexual abuse, only 35% of those in the Americas do. Even in countries where there are legal restrictions for marriage, it is not universally accepted that child marriage is sexual abuse. What is also surprising is that child prostitution is not universally accepted as abuse (in Africa, 15% of respondents accept this behaviour). While most countries had legal definitions of child sexual abuse and exploitation and had either voluntary or mandatory reporting procedures, only about 50% had legal penalties for not reporting.

Arrests in the prior year of the survey, related to child sexual abuse and exploitation, occurred in about 75% of countries, and only 50% of the victims received mental health support. The lack of support and treatment for victims is perhaps one of the most important gap areas worldwide and is not only restricted to less developed countries. Only 22% of countries have treatment programmes for victims of sexual abuse. Most of these programmes were aimed at the children and very few were aimed at the perpetrators.

Although there were well developed standardised treatments for sexual abuse, they were not often used in many countries.

RISK FACTORS FOR SEXUAL ABUSE

Child sexual abuse tends to occur within families and the perpetrators are often known to the child. However, with the advent of the internet and globalisation, even strangers can "groom" a child from considerable distance. Usually, there is a period for the perpetrator to cultivate a relationship with the child, which does not have to be sexual in nature. Rather, it takes the form of befriending and gaining of trust, both from the child as well as other adults in the family. Over time, the nature of the relationship turns sexual when the perpetrator begins to engage in sexual activities which eventually become anal, vaginal and/or digital penetration. The child might be made to believe that these activities are normal or part of a game, or that there was agreement and consent. Some perpetrators have claimed that they were trying to "educate" the child about sex before he or she learnt it from others.

During the abuse, the perpetrator may ignore the feelings of the child and may even act as though they do not exist. They may also physically or emotionally abuse the child, threaten them to keep the secret and force them to submit to an act.

Because of the secret nature of sexual abuse and the power the perpetrators have over the child, disclosure is often slow and sometimes accidental. Sometimes, it only occurs many years later when the victim is grown up. Many studies have shown that fewer than 50% of victims disclosed the abuse at the time it occurred (Lemaigre et al 2017). Many victims only revealed it much later in their lives when they were interviewed for the studies.

Certain factors are found to increase the risk of child sexual abuse:

- Victims tend to be weaker in some aspect or other, compared to the perpetrator.
- Victims are more likely to be younger children, although teenagers are also at increased risk as their sexuality becomes more obvious.
- Many victims are girls, although boys are being sexually abused as well. In the US, the often quoted figure is 1 in 4 girls, and 1 in 6 boys have been sexually abused.
- Disabled children or teenagers, who are less able to protect themselves and also less likely to reveal the abuse due to communication difficulties, have a higher risk of becoming victims.
- Absence of one or both parents due to parental separation, divorce or death. In some families, a parent is either physically or emotionally absent due to physical or mental illness.
- Presence of non-familial parent in the home, such as a stepfather or mother's boyfriend.
- Presence of abused siblings.
- Poverty, overcrowding and disorganised family system at home.
- Parental personality difficulties, e.g. antisocial personality.
- Serious marital conflicts, especially where the mother becomes sexually unavailable.

- Parental substance abuse.
- Social isolation with little support. Sometimes the perpetrator may deliberately isolate the family to maintain the abuse.

CONSEQUENCES OF CHILDHOOD SEXUAL ABUSE

Childhood sexual abuse can impact the child in the short term. They can also lead to serious chronic adult difficulties.

The effects of childhood sexual abuse depend on a number of factors:

- How the sexual abuse occurred. An acute sexual assault involving physical injury and sexual abuse involving genital penetration and more invasive forms of molestation (e.g. oral sex) is more likely to have a greater impact on the child. Abuse involving a care-giving adult is more traumatic as it involves betrayal of the child's trust. Chronic or frequent abuse, which occurs over a period of time, will be more harmful.
- The child's characteristics such as the temperament, emotional maturity and age.
- Family functioning and the presence of support.
- Other stressors in the child's life.

SHORT-TERM EFFECTS

These effects can occur immediately following the abusive incidents, and the child may develop emotional and behavioural problems, problems relating to others, and learning difficulties.

- Anxiety symptoms such as fearfulness, panic attacks and sleep disturbances (e.g. nightmares and insomnia) might occur. Fearfulness where the child avoids people, situations or places reminding him of the abuse may occur. Rarely, the child may appear to become lost and unable to remember who she is and what she was doing. This dazed state is called a hysterical fugue.

- Depressive symptoms (low mood, loss of appetite and sleep, poor concentration and suicidal ideations and attempts) might occur.

- Post-traumatic stress disorder (PTSD) might occur immediately or be delayed by a short period of time. Sexually abused children appear more likely to develop PTSD symptoms, which are characterised by heightened vigilance, avoidance of situations in which the trauma occurred and fearful re-experiencing of the traumatic events.

- Behavioural problems might occur in the form of running away from home, truancy, mixing with undesirable peers and getting involved in drugs, alcohol or even prostitution. Some of these maladaptive behaviours are understandable, given the family circumstances the victim lives in. Some victims may abuse alcohol or drugs as these help to temporarily numb the emotional pain of abuse. They may also overeat, believing that looking unattractive would help prevent further abuse. However, often these dysfunctional behaviours easily elicit negative reactions and judgemental attitudes from others, who may then take a punitive attitude instead of helping to uncover and ease the child's hidden distress.

- Precocious or increased sexualised behaviour may occur as a result of childhood sexual abuse. Hence, a sexually abused child may try to initiate adult-like sexual activity with her peers or other adults, and/or may engage in excessive self-masturbation. A sexually teenaged girl may become promiscuous as a result of her traumatic sexualisation. Such sexualised behaviour may then elicit stigmatisation, rejection, punishment, and even further abuse.

- Thinking processes may be affected by sexual abuse. These include self-blame, guilt, shame, loss of trust in others, and a sense of hopeless and helplessness which can affect the child's self-esteem, sense of self-competency and view of the world and the future. These feelings may be further reinforced by stigmatisation.

- The child may perform poorly in school due to poor concentration and preoccupation with the abuse. Depression and withdrawal from the environment and abuse-related anger leading to disruptive behaviour in class can lead to academic decline.

LONG-TERM EFFECTS

Child sexual abuse can lead to significant long-term effects that can continue in adulthood. These effects on adulthood are not so predictable; some survivors report very few effects while others may suffer from overwhelming abuse-related difficulties. Essentially, they can be summed up in four main areas:

1. **Emotional disturbance** such as depression, anxiety and anger can occur as long-term sequelae of childhood sexual abuse. Depression is the most commonly reported symptom with a fourfold greater lifetime risk of depression in sexual abuse victims than in individuals with no abuse history. The psychological mechanisms that occur in the acute stage becomes chronic and hard to treat. Victims of childhood sexual abuse may also experience generalised anxiety disorder, obsessive-compulsive disorder and somatisation disorders including developing headaches, stomach-aches and muscle tension. Victims of sexual abuse have been reported to have chronic irritability and unexpected rage towards the self or others. Some might engage in self-injurious behaviour, binging or purging to deal with intense emotional pain. Although these activities cause temporary relief, they are often followed by self-loathing and guilt, and becomes maladaptive repetitive behaviours. PTSD symptoms can persist into adulthood with the victim re-experiencing the abuse. Some survivors might experience psychological numbness with loss of memory about the traumatic events. They may

experience a feeling of being out-of-body and re-experience the trauma in a dream-like state. This can be a psychological defence against the pain of the trauma. Borderline personality disorder might develop, especially in girls. This is a personality problem in which the individual cannot regulate her emotions and is unable to develop stable relationships.

2. **Sexual difficulties**. Interpersonal difficulties might arise from childhood sexual abuse. Betrayal leading to lack of trust in others, emotional distress such as depression and anxiety, and post traumatic disorder and other maladaptive behaviours associated with abuse, can interfere with the survivor's ability to relate positively with others. Female victims might remain single, become promiscuous, or have marital difficulties. Not surprisingly, survivors might develop sexual difficulties in the form of revulsion for sex, frigidity or sexual dysfunction. There is also an increased risk of re-victimisation by abusive spouses or partners.

3. **Parenting difficulties**. Survivors may have difficulties raising their own children because of the impact on their mental health as well as emotional dysregulation that makes them inconsistent and at risk of being permissive or overly strict parents.

4. **Social problems**. Drug and alcohol abuse is a common result of childhood sexual abuse. These substances are used by the victim to numb the painful affects and memories associated with the abuse and it can become a persistent maladaptive response.

MANAGEMENT OF CHILD SEXUAL ABUSE

The management of child sexual abuse involves a multi-disciplinary team, which can comprise paediatricians, child psychiatrists, psychologists, social workers, the police and child protection workers. The assistance of schoolteachers may be needed to ensure that the child is safe from abuse. There should be regular sharing of information pertaining to the child and his family amongst the different professionals.

Mandatory reporting is not compulsory in every country, but most would have laws that support reporting of child sexual abuse to either the police or child welfare agencies. When reporting, the personal details of the child and parents or caregivers, place of residence and the details of the abuse should be given. This should also include information on whether the child is in immediate danger or needs urgent medical attention. The name of the school or child care centre or any other person who knows about the child's situation should also be provided for investigation.

The key issue during investigation is to determine if the child needs to be removed to a place of safety where the risk of further abuse is reduced e.g. hospital admission. Although this is often a difficult task and can be quite sudden and traumatic for the child, it still has to be done if the child's safety is at stake. It is usually better if the process is done with parental consent as the successful management of the child requires a good working relationship with the parents.

The victim requires a thorough assessment that includes the abuse situation and its possible causes, the strengths and weaknesses in the family, and the parents'/caregiver's willingness and ability to prevent further abuse. If there are other children in the family, it is also necessary to assess if they have been abused as well.

The child and family are provided with necessary social support and counselling if the risk of further abuse is minimal and the possibility of positive change and response to intervention is high. If this is not possible due to serious family issues, parental mental illness or high risk of further abuse, the child should be moved to a relative's, a foster parent's or a children's home. Even in these situations, effort should be made to work with the child and the family, with a plan to eventually return home. However, in very serious cases, permanent separation might be required and work has to be done to deal with the child's grief and other adjustments.

If you suspect child sexual abuse, take the following actions:

- Interview the child in a safe and private area.
- Encourage the child to explain what has happened in his/her own words. Do not become too emotional, but respond in an empathic way. Do not ask leading questions and do not make it an interrogation. Detailed interviewing of victims should be best left to the police and investigating professionals who have special protocols for doing so. However, if an adult is clarifying what the child is saying, it is best to ask open-ended questions and let the child narrate what is happening. For example, do not ask, "Did Uncle X touch your private parts?" Ask instead, "Has anyone done anything to make you feel uncomfortable?"
- Reassure the child that you believe them and they

should not be blamed. Do not make any promises you
cannot keep, e.g. that you will not tell anyone.

- Find out how to report what you have heard to the
relevant authorities which is often the child welfare
services (child protection agency) and/or the police.

Child protection agencies will then make an evaluation
as to the risk the child faces and whether the child can be at
home or placed in a safe environment. Specific removal of
the child sometimes depends on what symptoms the child
is exhibiting as admission to a residential facility has its pros
and cons. In addition, the offender may be removed from
the home of the child as well. Most of these interventions
by agencies at this point is for short-term protection of the
child. There is a need to then consider what supports and
collaborations are needed to protect the child in the long
term and commence a healing process.

Helping the child starts with identifying a case manager.
This is a professional usually with either nursing, social work
or psychology backgrounds to monitor the child, link them
to services as needed and assess ongoing needs.

Next is helping the child and family deal with the trauma of
sexual abuse which can be summarised in the following steps:

- Engaging the child in talking therapies (also known as
psychotherapy). The best evidence for efficacy is called
trauma focused cognitive behaviour therapy.
  - Psychoeducation involves helping the child understand
  what happens when trauma occurs and what needs to
  be done to help.
  - Relaxation techniques are taught.

– Emotion regulation is taught.

– Helping the child to understand what their thoughts are and how these affect how they feel.

– Talking about the actual traumatic incident in detail to help the child understand his negative thoughts and how to use them to deal with bad feelings.

– Meet with the parents to process the training.

– Teach the child self help safety skills.

- Additional support in school and family is often needed.

PREVENTION OF CHILD SEXUAL ABUSE

It is difficult to totally protect children from others and it is important that children are taught skills to protect themselves. Here are three simple principles to teach children, by Dr. Stanton Jones, a psychology professor:

- **Your body is private**. Children must be made aware that no one should be allowed to touch them without their permission especially the parts covered by a swimsuit. This refers not only to strangers, but also to people that they know.

- **Do not keep secrets**. Every child must know that they should not keep secrets and no one should ask them to keep secrets either.

- **Trust your feelings**. If the child feels that something which has happened to them is wrong, he or she should tell his or her parents. Children must not allow anyone to do things to them which do not feel right.

REFERENCES

Dubowitz, H., Bornes, N., & Tummala, P. (2016). *World perspectives on child abuse* (12th ed.).

Lemaigre C., Taylor E.P., & Gittoes C. (2017) *Barriers and facilitators to disclosing sexual abuse in childhood and adolescence: A systematic review.* In *Child Abuse and Neglect*, Vol. 70, 25.05.2017, p. 39-52.

Ministry of Social and Family Development, Singapore (2016). *Protecting Children in Singapore.*

World Health Organization (2017) www.who.int/mediacentre/factsheets/fs241/en/ accessed July 13, 2017.

World Health Organization and International Society for Prevention of Child Abuse and Neglect (2006). *Preventing child maltreatment: a guide to taking action and generating evidence.* http://apps.who.int/iris/bitstream/10665/43499/1/9241594365_eng.pdf

ABOUT THE AUTHORS

EIRLIANI ABDUL RAHMAN is Executive Director of a not-for-profit group, YAKIN (Youth, Adult survivors & Kin In Need), which seeks to help child victims and adult survivors of child sexual abuse. She is also Director at the Kailash Satyarthi Children's Foundation founded by the Nobel Peace Prize laureate. In September 2015, the #FullStop to #childsexualabuse campaign that Eirliani led on behalf of Kailash Satyarthi reached 16 million people over six weeks. Eirliani edited Satyarthi's book *Will for Children*, a collection of essays on child labour, published in December 2016. She also sits on Twitter's Trust & Safety Council. Eirliani writes for the *Huffington Post* and *DailyO*, the online platform of the Indian Today Group, on the issues of child abuse and child online safety.

A graduate of the London School of Economics and Warwick University, Eirliani is an avid rock climber and mountaineer, and currently resides in Colorado, USA.

DR. DANIEL FUNG is a child psychiatrist at the Institute of Mental Health's Child Guidance Clinic and Chairman of the Medical Board of Singapore's Institute of Mental Health. He graduated from the National University of Singapore's Faculty of Medicine in 1990 and obtained a Masters of Medicine in Psychiatry in 1996 and was awarded the Singapore Psychiatric Association Book prize. Dr. Fung is an Adjunct Associate Professor at the Yong Loo Lin Medical School, Duke-NUS Medical School, National University of Singapore and Lee Kong Chian School of Medicine, Nanyang Technological University.

He is currently the Vice President of the International Association for Child and Adolescent Psychiatry and Allied Professions and the Immediate Past President of the Asian Society of Child and Adolescent Psychiatry and Allied Professions.

Since the start of his career, Dr. Fung has been involved with working with children who have been abused and is active with the Singapore Children's Society where he received their Platinum Service Award in 2017. As a Principal Investigator and Co-Investigator for various studies involving innovative clinical interventions on disruptive behaviour disorders and anxiety disorders, his research is supported by the National Medical Research Council and other funding agencies. Dr. Fung has been involved in over 10 national-level funded research grants. He has co-authored over 100 peer reviewed research papers (88), books (30) and book chapters (18). Dr. Fung is also the programme director of REACH (Response, Early interventions and Assessment in Community mental Health), a community-based mental health programme in Singapore.